Cooking:
BASIC PRINCIPLES AND PROCEDURES

By:

David Miles

Sarah Miles

Legal deposit – Bibliothèque et Archives nationales du Québec, 2010
Legal deposit – Library and Archives Canada, 2010

ISBN 978-2-923623-26-9

Printed in Canada

Catalog Number: TAPD2

Authors:
David Miles
Sarah Miles

Editor-in-Chief:
Claude P. Major, Ph.D.

Copy Editors:
Krista Garver
Joanne Labre
Matthew Testa

Project Manager:
Francine Hébert, M. Ed.

Cover:
Jason Carrière

Design and Layout:
Michael Gonzalez
Natacha Lavigne
Rasha Razzak

Table of Contents

INTRODUCTION

The Modern Food Service Industry is an exciting, eclectic, and growing industry. A new interest in professional cooking as a career has emerged following the popularity of television cooking shows and culinary magazines. The attention has elevated many chefs to celebrity status. Food trends, dining, and culinary personalities have become popular with the masses, causing tremendous growth in the profession. Opportunity abounds for newly trained culinary professionals as the number of food service establishments continues to grow. Educated consumers are demanding quality, value, variety, and entertainment in their dining experiences. The industry is diverse, with both large corporations and small entrepreneurial businesses. Chefs from neighborhood bistros, corporate chefs, and celebrity chefs are all receiving respect for their valuable contributions to our way of life. It is a great time to begin a career in the food service industry!

Professional cooks need to be knowledgeable about many different things. They need to be familiar with the ingredients they use, the utensils they cook with, and the kitchen they work in. They need to know a wide variety of cooking methods and the effects of each method on the finished dish. They need to know how to follow a recipe and how to improvise without one. They need to be able to prepare everything from appetizers to desserts, and they need to make every dish tasty and attractive.

In this book, we will focus on some of the most fundamental skills and knowledge that any kitchen professional should possess. This information includes how a restaurant kitchen is organized, how to be professional and safe in the kitchen, and how to follow a recipe. This book also provides an overview of the most common cooking methods, preparations, and seasonings. In addition, you will find out how to prepare some of the most essential stocks and sauces, which are essential components of many of more advanced dishes.

▪ Chapter 1

Influences on Modern Cuisine

Modern food service practices are significantly linked to the industry's history, in that many techniques and culinary practices that are used in today's food service industry have evolved from centuries of tradition. Culinary techniques have been learned and then passed from teacher to apprentice for over a century. Today's culinary trends are influenced by the culinary history and traditions of many countries around the world. Modern cuisine is a blend of all these influences.

There are six major factors that will have affected a country's culinary history:

Availability of Food for the Population

▪ What food is available locally? What plants are natural to the area? What animals are abundant? What is available at the marketplace, including imports?

Climate

▪ How does the weather affect the food supply? Is extreme weather common, causing famine or droughts? Are multiple seasons a factor in food production?

Politics

▪ Has politics affected immigration in the area? Were regulations or taxes imposed affecting how the population ate?

Religion

- Did customs or rituals determine specific eating patterns in the population? Were certain foods forbidden to the population for religious reasons?

Culture

- How did the population's wealth affect their ability to afford certain foods? How did their lifestyle affect their choices in food?

Technology

- Has the evolution of technology affected the foods available to the population? Has technology changed the food production practices in the area?

The culinary history of France has influenced modern cuisine in a significant way. France's culinary history is important in that French chefs are accredited with documenting and developing in detail the culinary practices that we still use today.

History of the Restautant

Today's dining establishments are known as *restaurants*. The meaning of the word, to restore, comes from the French word *restaurer*. The earliest restaurants appeared around 1765 and were establishments that sold nutritional soups to weary travelers. A Parisian named Boulanger sold soups called **restoratives** that were widely believed to improve your health and energy levels. He is therefore credited with the first restaurant.

Restaurants similar to what we experience today began to emerge after the French revolution in 1793. Prior to the revolution professional chefs worked exclusively for the nobility. Their jobs were to prepare elaborate multicourse banquets. Common people had very few options for meals outside of their own home. At the time of the revolution, commoners put an end to the monarchy and many noble families came to an untimely death upon the guillotines. The professional chefs found themselves unemployed and needed to change the industry in a drastic way. At this point in history, many professional chefs became entrepreneurs and opened their own businesses in the form of restaurants. Culinary history was changed forever. It became fashionable to eat out if you could afford it. By the 19th century, dining out had become a habit of the upper class as well as the middle class. Restaurants were offering diners meal choices, and the concept of customer service was born. At the time, leading restaurants offered a vast selection of choices with as many as 12 soups, 65 main dishes, and 50 desserts!

Notable French Chefs

There were two notable chefs in the history of French cuisine. Marie Antoine (Antonin) Carême was perhaps the most important chef of his time. He was born in 1784 and began working in kitchens at the age of 10. By the time he was a young man, he had apprenticed in all aspects of the kitchen. He became interested in documenting the culinary techniques and practices of his time. He managed to publish a reference textbook, the first of its kind, detailing every aspect of culinary techniques and principles. He was widely known as the "cook of kings and the king of cooks." He was famous for his elaborate banquet sculptures in sugar and ice. For these reasons he is considered the founder of Classic Cuisine, the basis on which our current practices are formed. During his short lifetime of only 50 years, he managed to publish many culinary reference books, leaving us a solid understanding of culinary practices of that time.

Antonin Carême (1784–1833)

The second notable chef, Auguste Escoffier, built upon the work of Chef Carême. Escoffier, born in 1846, was a highly successful and celebrated chef

Auguste Escoffier (1846–1935)

of his time. He designed a system of organization for professional kitchens, which is still in use today. He implemented and tested his theories of kitchen organization in many distinguished hotel kitchens of the time, including the Ritz Hotel in Paris. His system used a brigade of chefs divided into stations, which streamlined kitchen practices. He is also responsible for simplifying the lengthy menus of the time. He published many culinary reference books. Current practices have evolved since his time; however, his teachings are still evident in today's kitchens.

Since that time, many changes and improvements have been made in kitchen practices. Countless chefs, authors, and cooking schools have built upon the teachings of these two pioneers of professional cooking. Modern food service practices have evolved significantly. Technology has made a significant impact. Many new machines have been invented to aid in the production of food. Advances in technology allow these machines to be powered by gas or electricity.

Motorized tools have simplified many tasks in the kitchen and reduced production times. Modern refrigeration has enabled improvements in the distribution of food, making rare ingredients more available. Centralized production has been made possible through developments in packaging and freezing. Advances in health sciences have altered how we view and handle ingredients.

Today's food service industry includes many different types of operations. Major types of food service operations can be broadly categorized into the following:

Restaurants
- Fast Food/Convenience
- Fine Dining
- Casual Dining
- Take-out
- Hotel Kitchens

Institutional Kitchens
- Hospitals
- Schools
- Military Mess Halls
- Correctional Institutions
- Transportation Production Kitchens
- Corporate Kitchens

Catering Establishments
- Corporate
- Private
- Fast Food Delivery

Food Product Manufacturing Kitchens
- Production Kitchens
- Test Kitchens
- Food Styling Kitchens

There are many more subcategories within this framework of food service establishments. Their common factor is the need for skilled culinary artisans to be successful.

Chapter 1
Questions...

1) Which of the following is true?

   a. The food service business is on the decline.
   b. The marketplace has more educated consumers than ever before.
   c. Chefs are not respected in the community.

2) Name three factors that could have affected your country's culinary history.

   Population   Climate   Politics   Religion   culture   Technology

3) What country has had the most influence on modern culinary practices?

   France

4) Restaurants as we know them today emerged after what great event in history?

   a. World War II
   b. The War of 1812
   c. The French Revolution

5) Antonin Carême is credited with _____ .

   a. documenting culinary practices
   b. founding of classic cuisine
   c. creating sugar and ice sculptors
   d. all of the above

6) Name the famous chef who created and implemented the "kitchen brigade."

   auguste Escoffier

Chapter 2

Kitchen Organization

Food service operations usually have a team of professionals to complete the necessary tasks. Anywhere from two to a hundred or more workers can be found in a typical food service facility. In a kitchen environment there are many dangers and pressures; therefore, effective and efficient organization is mandatory.

The Kitchen Brigade

A kitchen team is called a **brigade**. A kitchen brigade is organized by levels of authority similar to a military system. At each level of authority, responsibilities are delegated and fulfilled by the subordinate members of the team. Work orders are given from the top of the chain of command, and tasks are delegated down to each level in the chain. Every individual is given a specific and identifiable area of responsibility and is supervised by the person higher in the chain of command. This is the system invented by Chef Escoffier, and it is still used in most professional kitchens today.

In the kitchen, the highest level in the chain of command is the **executive chef**, who is in charge of the entire kitchen operations and is held accountable by senior management and business owners for the kitchen's success. The executive chef is responsible for planning the menus, controlling costs and revenues, organizing and directing the staff, and

preparing detailed reports for management. The position of executive chef comes with great responsibility, and is an exciting and stressful position. If the team is successful, the executive chef will be rewarded; if unsuccessful, the executive chef must take full responsibility.

Next in the chain of command are the **sous chefs**. Sous chefs report directly to the executive chef and are responsible for carrying out the daily tasks in the kitchen. They are supervisors to the station chefs, cooks, and general laborers. They must ensure all food is produced correctly and efficiently. Sous chefs usually work in the kitchen and often participate in the food production. In smaller operations, there may be only one sous chef. In larger operation, each sous chef is in charge of a different shift in the kitchen. All sous chefs ensure that the tasks outlined by the executive chef are completed as directed. If the executive chef is not in the kitchen or is away from the premises, the sous chef must make

decisions. Sous chefs must be leaders, teachers, and coaches. They must manage, motivate, and train many chefs and cooks under their charge. Sous chefs must carry out the executive chef's wishes even if they might prefer to do things differently. It is a position with great responsibility, but little glory, as the executive chef will get the praise for the team's success.

Chefs de partie (also called **station chefs**), report to the sous chef. Each chef de partie has a defined area of responsibility called a **station**. The sous chef gives each chef de partie a list of tasks to carry out for his or her station. Each chef de partie might have to supervise cooks and general laborers assigned to his or her station. The station chef first completes all tasks required to prepare the station for service. At the time of service they supervise orders from their station and ensure they are fulfilled properly. Station chefs are responsible at all times for a clean and organized station. Any difficulties in carrying out their orders are reported to the sous chef.

All stations in the kitchen are manned by **cooks**, who assist the station chefs and sous chefs in carrying out their assigned tasks. Cooks are skilled workers who are gaining experience in the kitchen. They are rotated through the kitchen operations and assigned to each of the stations in order to learn the required skills towards becoming a chef. Cooks are expected to respect the chefs who supervise them and must learn a variety of skills from each of their chef mentors.

General kitchen workers perform tasks such as arranging inventory, garbage detail, cleaning, or washing dishes. Many of these positions can lead to a promotion to cook once a worker has proven his or her dedication and ability to work hard. Not all kitchens have such staff. In many kitchens, the cooks and chefs must do their own cleaning and dishwashing.

Kitchen Stations

In today's kitchens, the executive chef is responsible for planning the various stations. The executive chef will analyze the projected number of customers the establishment expects to be serving, the physical limits of the kitchen, and the planned menu in order to determine what stations will be necessary. Chef Escoffier invented the system of stations used in traditional kitchens:

Garde Manger / PANTRY CHEF
"guard monjay"
- Salads, dressings, cold starters

Rôtisseur / ROASTING CHEF
"row tee sur"
- roasted meats, gravy

Entremetier / VEGETABLE CHEF
"on tra met yay"
- vegetables, soups, eggs

Grillardin / GRILL CHEF
"grill ar dan"
- grilled meats, broiled meats

Saucier / SAUCE CHEF
"saw see ay"
- sauces, stews, sauté meats

Poissonier / FISH CHEF
"pwa sun yay"
- fish, shellfish

Pâtissier / PASTRY AND DESSERT CHEF
"pat ees yay"
- pastries, desserts

Tournant / REPLACEMENT CHEF
"tour non"
- any station where required

Every kitchen establishment has a variation of this system depending on the size, menu, and facilities. The system exists to establish clear and concise levels of responsibility and authority in order to aid in effective operations. In small food-service establishments, one chef may have to look after all of the stations. In large operations, the stations can be responsible for one specific task, one specific menu item, or a whole area in the kitchen. The system is respected by chefs, cooks, and workers for creating order, and it has proven to be effective for over a century.

OUTLINE OF THE KITCHEN SYSTEM

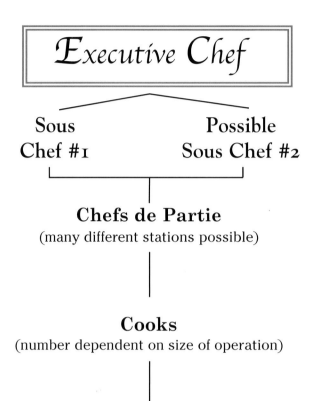

Executive Chef

Sous
Chef #1

Possible
Sous Chef #2

Chefs de Partie
(many different stations possible)

Cooks
(number dependent on size of operation)

General Laborers
(number dependent on size of operation)

Chapter 2
Questions...

1. True or False:

    A kitchen team is referred to as a "Troop."

2. What is an executive chef responsible for?

    a. planning menus
    b. directing the staff
    c. controlling food costs
    d. all of the above

3. What is another name for chef de partie?

    Station chef

4. If the executive chef is away from the kitchen, who takes over the responsibilities of operations?

    sous chef

5. Which of the following statements about cooks is true?

    a. Cooks are untrained laborers.
    b. Cooks must go to school to learn to be a cook.
    c. Cooks are not required to wash dishes.
    d. none of the above

6. Name three traditional stations from Chef Escoffier's kitchen brigade.

Chapter 3

Standards of Professionalism

Kitchen professionals have a specific work ethic that is distinct from many other working professionals. It has developed out of necessity due to the unique environment of a professional kitchen as well as from traditions in the culinary profession. The expected standards are often unwritten, but they exist in most professional operations. It is important to learn these standards and to govern yourself accordingly, and to understand why the standards exist.

Ethics

A chef is expected to

- Be dedicated to the goals of the operation
- Take pride in his or her work
- Be a willing participant
- Work in a clean and safe manner
- Take responsibility for his or her work
- Be ambitious
- Take constructive criticism
- Be willing to improve
- Be willing to practice
- Be willing to invest time in learning
- Understand the consequences of lack of attendance
- Be a team member

A successful kitchen brigade will definitely be working with these ethics in place. All members of the team respect this code of ethics, so the

kitchen is as safe and organized as possible. They take pride in doing a great job. If they do make mistakes, they can address them and improve because they are dedicated to success. The kitchen will be busy, but the atmosphere will be calm and pleasant because people treat each other, and their environment, with respect. The brigade can enjoy their successes together because they have worked hard and accomplished their goals.

Consider what would happen if these ideals didn't exist! Laziness would creep in and the products of the kitchen would look and taste awful; sickness could result due to unsanitary conditions. Chefs and cooks would be hurting themselves and causing delays in delivering the product to the customer. Everyone would be stressed out and angry at each other, and the team would start to fall apart. Not a recipe for success!

Skills Required for Success as a Kitchen Professional

Chefs and cooks require obvious skills to become successful, such as knowing how to cook and specific techniques; however, there are many other skills that are just as important for success in a culinary career. These skills are more abstract, and sometimes they are the hardest to learn. There are two categories of these skills:

1) Interpersonal and communication skills

2) Physical and mental skills

Interpersonal and Communication Skills

Interpersonal skills are required for efficiency and safety in the kitchen. Chefs are required to speak precisely and clearly. Misunderstanding can cause confusion and delays in output, as well as accidents. Consider the difference between these two communications and the possible outcomes:

1) "Take this over there."

2) "Take this pot of boiling water and carefully pour it into the sink."

The receiver of message 1 might not understand that the water is boiling hot and could burn him!

You must show respect in the kitchen, for others and for their belongings. This will prevent situations from brewing between workers that cause disagreements and arguments. In an environment where there is a lot of pressure, heat and strong personalities can sometimes make it difficult for people to hold their emotions in check. Controlling your temper, showing self-control, and taking responsibility for your actions are qualities that are necessary in this career path. A chef or cook who leaves a station, displays a bad temper, or disobeys a superior could be dismissed on the spot!

As a kitchen professional you must learn to

- Show respect for superiors

- Communicate clearly and precisely

- Be honest with yourself and others

- Learn self-control

- Be polite and considerate

- Be respectful of others' belongings

- Take criticism in a constructive manner

- Take full responsibility for your actions

Once you have mastered these skills, you will be able to handle any situation that arises in the kitchen calmly and skillfully, and others will appreciate having you on their team.

Physical and Mental Skills

A professional cooking career is exciting and rewarding. It can also be challenging in ways you may not realize. Working in any kitchen requires a great deal of physical exertion. Lifting, stirring, chopping, carrying boxes, and more, all require energy and physical strength. A shift in the kitchen can be compared to an intensive workout at the gym! It is a workout both physically and mentally. To prosper in this environment, you must accept this reality and govern yourself accordingly.

Many shifts in the kitchen are long and tiring. Labor laws have changed this somewhat, but reality in the kitchen dictates the actual end of shifts. The kitchen brigade cannot leave before dessert is served at the end of an event just because a shift is supposed to end. Labor laws govern the length of shifts and breaks required, but reality is more closely linked with the tasks required to be completed by a certain deadline and by other dynamics. If dinner hour is approaching and the preparations are not completed, a chef will not likely grant a break until everything is ready for service. This is the way of the kitchen. It is the only way a team can achieve success.

The industry has historically been known for its supposed alcoholism and other addictions. This was caused by the long and late hours in the kitchen and the tremendous pressures. Today, this is not widely the case, and it is certainly not respected or common in today's kitchens. Labor laws and current thinking have changed this practice dramatically.

A kitchen can be very hot. Exposure to this heat over many hours can dehydrate a worker, sometimes to the point of collapse. In order to avoid this, one must constantly drink water to keep hydrated. Kitchen professionals must learn their physical limits and get rest when necessary. A dedicated chef will ensure he or she is fully rested before a shift begins in order to have the stamina to make it through the entire shift.

Keeping yourself in good health is also of utmost importance. Absence from work has major consequences for a kitchen brigade. A kitchen brigade depends on its members to carry out their duties effectively and efficiently. A missing team member changes the dynamics of the team and places pressures on the team to complete more work within the same amount of time. If absence is necessary, advance notice to the chef is imperative so that a replacement chef can be scheduled. How you govern yourself in your attendance matters very much to the team and to your superiors. This is an issue that chefs take very seriously, perhaps more so than people in other occupations. Dedicated chefs do not abandon their station unless they are seriously incapacitated. A pattern of absence could mean a demotion or dismissal.

A kitchen brigade wears traditional uniforms in the kitchen. Professional kitchen workers show up for work in a clean and proper uniform designed for safety and cleanliness. They must understand the requirements for good grooming and hygiene for kitchen professionals, as this has an impact on success. Would you eat at a restaurant where the kitchen help looked dirty and had hair hanging down into the soup you had ordered? You would probably find this unacceptable. The perception of cleanliness is paramount to a successful operation.

Mental stamina and the ability to act rationally under stress and deal with fatigue are all mental skills that chefs must work at to achieve success. These skills may not come naturally to some, but being rested and maintaining a positive attitude will help you to cope in the kitchen environment.

Physical and mental skills that are helpful:

- Show up for work rested
- Positive attitude
- Cheerful disposition
- Commitment to good health
- Committed to good hygiene and grooming
- Cleanliness in work habits
- Clean uniform
- Properly attired
- Good stamina
- Willingness to learn and improve

A Typical Uniform in the Kitchen

Almost all professional kitchens maintain the practice of traditional uniforms. Many kitchens have a uniform service that launders and presses all of the uniforms and delivers them for use on a rotating basis. This eliminates the possibility of variations in dress and cleanliness. The workers always have what they need for their shift.

Chef Jacket

Chef jackets are usually made of white cotton. The design of the jacket has a cross-over front with large buttons for easy removal in case of a hot liquid spill. The buttons can be done on one side or the other so that there is always a clean front. Chef jackets usually have long sleeves to protect arms from spills and spatters. A long narrow pocket on the upper sleeve holds a pen and a thermometer. Chefs often have distinction medals pinned or sewn on their collar.

Chef Hat

Traditionally, chef hats were made of cotton, but now they are often made of disposable paper or breathable lightweight fabric. They are cylindrical with vertical folds. The taller the hat, the higher the rank. Traditional chef hats have 52 folds, representing the number of ways to cook an egg.

Cook's Hat

Today's cooks wear a variety of different headwear ranging from baseball hats to skull caps, but traditionally they wore a boat-shaped cap. These caps are not popular today.

Some cooks wear a floppy version of a chef hat that is more commonly known as a baker's hat.

Chef's and Cook's Pants

Chefs always wear black or dark blue pants with an elastic waist for comfort and easy removal in case of a hot liquid spill. Cooks have traditionally worn the same, but with a navy houndstooth pattern. It is becoming normal for chef's and cook's pants to have more patterns, and today's catalogues present a variety of colorful options.

Apron

A chef's apron is long and wide to completely wrap around the waist. They often have a bib, which many chefs roll down. The apron strings wrap all the way around the body, and many chefs tuck utensils or towels there.

Towel

A supply of clean, lint-free towels is required for cleaning plate rims or spills.

Footwear

Chefs and cooks spend all day on their feet on floors that are often slippery. It is important to wear the appropriate footwear. Traditionally clogs were worn; however, a variety of comfortable non-skid work shoes are used today.

A properly dressed and groomed brigade instills confidence in the dining public. The perception is that a clean and groomed brigade must run a clean and sanitary kitchen, and therefore they have confidence in the abilities of the brigade to feed them in a safe and healthy manner. This perception is critical for a successful operation as diners will not return to a restaurant they perceive as being dirty or unhealthy.

Chapter 3
Questions...

1. Choose two interpersonal skills that help in the kitchen.

   a. be willing to learn
   b. be polite and considerate
   c. show respect for superiors
   d. show up clean and showered for work

2. True or False:

   It is important to be open to new ideas in the kitchen.

3. True or False:

   You can take a break any time you want to in a kitchen.

   g. et Rested   get clean   Good Grooming

4. What is something you can do to prepare yourself for work in a kitchen?

5. How many folds are on traditional chef hats, and what do the folds represent?

   52 the Number of way Can Cook an Egg

■ Chapter 4

The Safe Workplace and Injury Prevention

Kitchens are often hazardous environments with sharp knives, slippery floors, and hot liquids—all potentially dangerous or harmful. It is desirable in a professional kitchen to prevent these hazardous situations from causing any harm. Safety programs are required by law, and they are a necessity in all professional kitchens. Most safety programs focus on educating employees to work in a manner that promotes the prevention of accidents. Employees are also trained in first aid in order to help each other in any emergency situations. It is the responsibility of management to provide a safe environment for its workers. Clearly marked safety exits, fire extinguishers, first aid kits, safe wiring, adequate lighting, non-skid flooring, safety-tested equipment and barrier-free fire exits are all mandatory for a proper safety program. Once implemented, the safety program should be strictly adhered to.

To Prevent Burns:

- Warn other employees when approaching them with hot items
- Wear a proper uniform and non-skid shoes
- Never use a wet towel to handle a hot pan
- Keep all liquids away from the deep fryer area
- Use protective eyewear when using the deep fryer
- Stay clear of steam when opening hot containers or ovens
- Use protective oven mitts to handle hot pans
- Ask for help when lifting heavy items that are hot

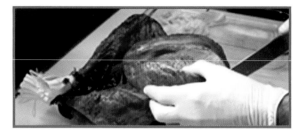

To Prevent Cuts

- Keep your equipment sharp; dull knives are more dangerous

- Use a plastic or wood cutting board, never metal

- Place a damp cloth under your cutting board to prevent it from sliding

- When walking with a knife in your hand, keep it in a protective sheath or walk with the point down and the sharp edge facing away from you

- Do not place knives in a sink full of soapy water where they may not be seen

- Do not pick up broken glass pieces with your hands, instead use a broom and dust pan

- Do not store glasses in the food preparation area

- Do not place broken plates or glasses in the garbage; use a specific bucket designated for this purpose

- Discard any chipped glasses or plates

- Be careful of sharp nails and staples in delivery boxes

- Store your knives on a magnetic rack or knife block

To Prevent Fires

- Do not allow smoking anywhere in the kitchen

- Keep all fire exits free of obstacles such as boxes or garbage

- Keep all equipment clean and grease-free

- Ensure all staff are well versed in fire procedures

- Never leave cooking unattended

- If alarm sounds, turn off all equipment immediately

To Prevent Falling

- Keep stairs and corridors free of obstacles such as boxes and garbage pails

- Wear proper non-skid shoes

- Walk slowly, and do not run in the kitchen

- Spread salt on temporary grease spills

- Salt frozen walkways

- Keep the floors clean and dry at all times

- Use proper step ladders to reach items on upper shelves

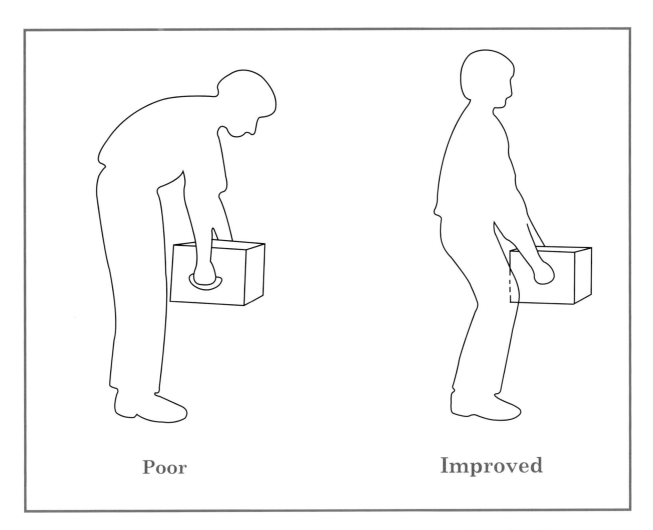

Poor   Improved

To Prevent Muscle Injuries

- Always use your legs to lift a heavy object, not just your back

- Keep your knees bent when lifting heavy items or leaning over counters

- Stretch your muscles before and often during a shift

- Alternate hands while doing repetitive tasks

Other Things You Can Do to Avoid Injury

- Be knowledgeable about first aid procedures

- Be knowledgeable about operating all equipment available to you

- Do not take unnecessary risks

- Use caution in all tasks

- Place large hot pots farther back on the stove top and small pots in the front

- Make sure all loose apron strings are secure before operating any machinery

Chapter 4 *The Safe Workplace and Injury Prevention*

Questions...
Chapter 4

1. Management in a professional kitchen should provide which of the following safety items?

   a. non-slip flooring
   b. healthy meals
   c. fire extinguishers
   d. bright lighting

2. Which of the following should be used to handle hot pans?

   a. wet towel
   b. dry oven mitt
   c. dry towel

3. Name two things you can do to prevent fires.

4. Name two things you can do to prevent muscle injuries.

5. When walking around the kitchen with a knife you should _____.

   a. carry it in a sheath
   b. carry it in front of you pointing out
   c. carry it beside you pointing down
   d. a and c

Chapter 5

Sanitation

In professional working kitchens it is possible to create situations where harmful or even deadly bacteria can grow and develop to a stage that could seriously harm workers or customers. Strict guidelines are created and must be followed to insure that these situations do not occur.

The study of the subject is called **sanitation** and refers to keeping a sanitary environment. *Sanitary* is a word that describes a clean, safe, and germ-free environment. The efforts of a sanitation program are to prevent harmful bacteria from growing and spreading and also to prevent humans from passing harmful bacteria to one another.

Bacteria exist in all foods in small quantities. In order for bacteria to become harmful, they must grow and multiply. In order for bacteria to grow and multiply, they require warm temperatures, air, moisture, and time. The combination of these factors will allow the bacteria to multiply to a level that will cause humans to become sick. Sanitation programs are practiced in order to prevent this situation from occurring. Washing foods, monitoring temperatures of foods, and wrapping foods in protective plastic or containers are all examples of sanitation practices. Another goal of sanitation programs is to prevent bacteria from spreading. Humans can transfer bacteria to one another or to an object, for example, a cooking utensil. Sanitation programs help us to prevent bacteria from spreading using the Protocols of Personal Hygiene.

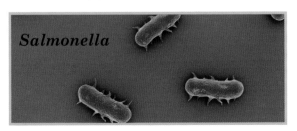

Salmonella

Protocols of Personal Hygiene

- Prior to your kitchen shift, take a shower and wash your hair

- Wear a hair net in the kitchen

- Wear a clean uniform and apron

- Do not go to work if you have a communicable infection or disease

- Wash your hands regularly using the proper sanitary method

Washing Your Hands

Washing your hands properly and frequently is the single most effective way to prevent the spread of harmful bacteria. It is necessary to wash your hands after touching raw meat or dairy, after sneezing or coughing, eating, smoking, touching your hair, and especially after using the washroom. In fact, most cooks' and chefs' hands are raw from washing so frequently. A common practice is to keep hand lotion beside the soap to apply after washing to help keep the skin from drying out.

Prevention: The Key to an Effective Sanitation Program

In order to prevent food contamination by harmful bacteria, we must implement safe food storage practices. Government Health and Safety Boards monitor food operations to ensure safe practices are in order. Safety boards issue guidelines for operators to follow, then send inspectors to make sure that the guidelines are being met. Perishable food items must be kept at cool temperatures in order to prevent them from developing harmful bacteria. Refrigerators are used to cool foods to the proper temperature. The

1 Wet your hands

2 Apply solution and scrub for at least 15 seconds

3 Scrub back of hands, wrists, between fingers, and under fingernails

4 Rinse your hands

5 Turn off water lever using your elbows

6 Dry with paper towel

danger zone (the temperature to avoid) is from 41°F to 140°F, or 5°C to 60°C, as this is the ideal temperature range for bacteria growth.

Food Storage

There are three types of food storage: refrigerated storage, freezer storage, and dry storage. The guidelines for storing food must be strictly adhered to at all times.

Refrigerated Storage

Perishable foods are items that will eventually spoil. These foods must be kept at a safe temperature between 32°F to 40°F, or 0°C to 4°C. Raw food items and cooked food items should be stored in separate containers and in separate areas of the fridge. Items should be stored in an organized manner. Each food item should be in a separate container and marked with the date on which it was first stored. This helps to prevent the use of an item that may have spoiled. Store food items that may drip on the bottom shelf of the fridge and be sure to maintain a clean fridge at all times. Monitor the temperature of the fridge regularly to be sure that it is in the correct temperature range. Do not overcrowd the fridge as this will cause poor air circulation. Do not leave food to rot in the fridge.

Freezer Storage

Foods stored in the freezer must be wrapped tightly in cling wrap to protect them from freezer burn. Freezers must be kept at 0°F (–18°C) or lower. Follow the same methods for storing foods as in the fridge. Do not leave foods endlessly in the freezer as the quality of foods diminish the longer they are frozen. Defrost frozen food slowly in the refrigerator. If in a hurry you can thaw under cold running water or in a microwave oven. Thawing items at room temperature can cause bacteria to develop on the outside of the item while the inside is still defrosting. Freezers must be turned off occasionally in order to be cleaned and sanitized.

Dry Storage

Many food items do not need to be refrigerated. These items are stored at room temperature in the dry storage area. Dry storage items should be kept on shelves in airtight containers at all times. Dry storage includes unopened cans and bottles as well as flour, sugar, cereals, spices, and oils. It is important to monitor the dry storage area to check for freshness as even dry items can lose quality over time.

Food Holding

Food holding describes keeping foods at a specific temperature. This is commonly done during service to keep food dishes at their appropriate serving temperature. Steam tables are widely used to perform this task. The temperature should remain above 140°F (60°C). Food items should be properly covered. The holding equipment should be preheated before the food is placed in it. The food should be heated to the proper temperature before placing it in the holding unit. Other food holding equipment is designed to keep foods cold during the service. Remember to keep foods covered and do not overfill containers as the food on the surface will not be chilled and bacteria could then develop on the surface.

Food Handling

Proper sanitation practices for handling and preparing foods must be strictly adhered to. All surfaces in the kitchen must be sanitized before, during, and after food preparation.

Before you begin your food preparation, it is advisable to sanitize your tools and work area to ensure cleanliness. While you are working with food, be sure to wash your hands and equipment after contact with any raw meat or dairy products. A consistent practice of cleaning after each task is a good habit to acquire. When you have finished your work, you must systematically clean and sanitize every piece of equipment that you used. Be thorough in this task. Disassemble any removable equipment parts, taking care to unplug any electrical equipment prior to doing this and clean all parts of the equipment. Make sure you are using clean cloths at all times. Cleaning a counter with a cloth infected with harmful bacteria from raw chicken is not helpful! A popular kitchen saying, "time to lean, time to clean," exemplifies the necessary attitude in a professional kitchen. To maintain a professional and sanitary environment, when not cooking, one must be cleaning.

Proper Dishwashing Procedure

Effective cleaning of dishes and cooking equipment is a three-step process that must be strictly adhered to.

Step One: Scraping and Rinsing

- Scrape any waste into a garbage pail

- Rinse in a sink of hot water

Step Two: Washing

- Equipment is washed in warm soapy water

- Hot water is sprayed to remove the suds

Step Three: Sanitizing and Drying

- All equipment is rinsed in a chemical or bleach sanitizer to kill germs. Some automatic machines sanitize by heat (180°F or 82°C)

- Dishes must be heat dried or drip dried before use

- Always make sure machine temperatures are monitored. Machines that sanitize with chemicals must be 140°F (60°C)

Pest Control

Proper sanitation practices include a pest control program. Most kitchen operations hire a professional company to perform prevention programs. A professional program usually includes monthly visits for inspection and the spraying of chemicals to keep insects at bay. Workers in the kitchen must practice preventive measures to keep unwanted visitors out of the kitchen.

- Inspect incoming supplies
- Store all supplies off the floor
- Keep floors, shelves, walls, and equipment clean at all times
- Keep all doors and windows closed or screened at all times
- Store garbage in proper containers with tight-fitting lids
- Store garbage containers in an enclosed area and remove as soon as possible to a dumpster

All professional kitchens implement programs for sanitation. Local health departments inspect all kitchens regularly to ensure the programs are being followed. It is important for all staff in a kitchen to be familiar with the procedures and to follow them strictly. Following these procedures will ensure good health for employees and customers. Any sloppiness in this area could seriously harm employees and diners. The health department may close operations for unsanitary practices, causing financial losses.

Chapter 5
Questions...

1. In order to grow, bacteria need _____.

   a. time
   b. air
   c. warm temperatures
   d. food
   e. moisture
   f. all of the above

2. Why is sanitation important?

   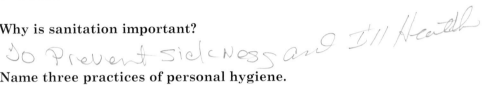
   To Prevent sickness and Ill Health

3. Name three practices of personal hygiene.

4. What is the single most important thing cooks and chefs can do to prevent the spread of harmful bacteria?

   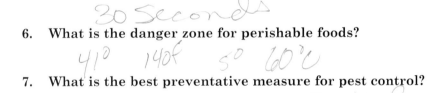
   Wash Hair Clean Uniform Wash Hands

5. How long should you wash your hands to clean them effectively?

   30 Seconds

6. What is the danger zone for perishable foods?

   41° 140f 5° 60°C

7. What is the best preventative measure for pest control?

   live a professional

Chapter 6

Tools and Equipment

Every kitchen has tools both large and small to assist the kitchen staff with their tasks. Some tools such as knives, pots, and pans have been used for centuries, and others are modern electric machines that perform larger tasks in larger quantities and in a timely manner. It is important for kitchen workers to understand the safe handling and operation of all kitchen tools. Hands-on training is the best method to learn proper techniques and safety practices. Large equipment can vary from one model to another; therefore, it is important to have a tutorial on the use of each kitchen machine before using it for the first time. Small kitchen equipment is referred to as **small wares**. Small tools require practice to use safely and efficiently. It is important to maintain tools properly to keep them safe and useful.

Knives

It is arguable that a chef or cook's most important tools are his or her hands. After that, most chefs and cooks would choose a knife as their most important tool. A wide range of knives in varying shapes and sizes are available. Varying degrees of quality affect the cost, weight, and feel of knives. It is best to try them first to make sure you like them before investing. For use in your own home kitchen, you may wish to invest in expensive high-quality knives, as they will last a lifetime. It is advisable to leave these expensive knives at home though, as bringing them to work could result in

a loss or a theft. Many professional kitchens have a knife service that delivers sharpened knives frequently on a rotating schedule. Other kitchens require you to provide your own set of knives. In this case it is advisable to purchase less expensive knives that are easily replaceable. A good chef's knife is the most important knife for a chef. This knife should feel like an extension of your hand with a comfortable grip and weight. All knives must be kept in a safe place in a manner where the blades do not touch each other. The knife-edge should be sharpened before each use. The following are standard knives (in alphabetical order) commonly used in the kitchen:

Boning Knife

Boning knives have slim and pointed blades that help to remove raw meat from bones. The point has a thin and curved tip. Most blades are flexible, but some are stiff for uses with heavier cuts of meat. Flexible blades are also used for filleting fish.

Chef's Knife

Chef's knives have wide tapered blades that are used for general-purpose tasks such as slicing or chopping. Typically they are 6, 8, or 10 inches in length.

Clam Knife

This is a short knife with a thick blade and rounded tip, used for opening clams.

Cleaver

Cleavers are heavy knives used to cut through bones. They have a thick rectangular blade and the flat side of the blade is also used to crush garlic and to pound meats.

Oyster Knife

These knives have short and pointed blades with one sharp edge. There is usually a hand guard between the knife blade and handle. The knife is wedged between the two halves of the oyster shell and twisted to open the shell. The sharp edge is then used to remove the oyster from the shell.

Paring Knife

Paring knives are used for small and precise tasks. The blades vary between 2 and 4 inches in length. They are often used to shape vegetables and fruits.

Salad Knife

This is a light knife with a long blade and pointed tip used to prepare leaf salads and sometimes fruit.

Serrated Knife

These knives are used for cutting soft items like bread, tomatoes, and fruit. They have long blades with scalloped edges. Longer serrated knives are often used for carving cooked meats.

How to Sharpen Knives

Professional sharpening services are available and it is advisable to have your knives professionally sharpened once in a while. Most chefs and cooks use a two-step method, stone and steel, to sharpen their knives. The method for sharpening is as follows:

- Wet your sharpening stone and place on a flat work surface

- Hold your knife with the tip of the blade pointing away from your body

- Hold the knife handle in your right hand with the blade horizontal and the sharp side of the blade facing the stone

- Place your available fingers on top of the flat side of the blade in order to help you guide the knife

- Hold the tip of the knife at the top right side of the stone and with the blade on the stone at a 20° angle

- Move the knife blade over the stone from right to left keeping a gentle even pressure on the blade

- As you move from right to left smoothly slide the knife from the tip to the base along the stone

- Repeat in exactly the same manner and always in the same direction until the blade is sharp

- Next repeat on the other side of the blade in the opposite direction until sharp

- Use a soft cloth to gently wipe the knife clean

- Next take the sharpening steel in your left hand away from your body

- Place your knife in your other hand with the base of the blade at the top of the steel at a 20° angle

- Gently pull down on your knife, running the blade of your knife from the base to the tip along the length of the steel

- Put the knife base behind the steel at the top at a 20° angle

- Run the knife along the steel from the base to the tip

- Repeat this motion several times on each side

- Wipe clean with a soft cloth

Your knife is now sharpened and ready to use.

Safe Handling of Your Knife

Safe handling of your knife is imperative, as serious injury to yourself or others is possible. Always use sharp knives, as dull knives are even more dangerous. Always use a cutting board. Place a wet towel under your cutting board to keep it from moving while you are working. Grip the handle of your knife in a manner that is comfortable. Some chefs prefer to keep their thumb on the blade of the knife while others use only the handle. Your free hand is used as a guide. Hold the item you want to cut, insuring your fingertips are rolled over to the first knuckle. As you cut, your knuckles will help you to know where your knife is while keeping your fingertips out of the way of the blade. The heavier base of the knife will assist you in cutting through thicker items. The center of the blade is used for general work, and the tip can assist you with precise cuts. Always sanitize your knives after use and store in a safe place and in a manner that protects the blades.

Small Wares

The following is a list of small wares that can be found in commercial kitchens:

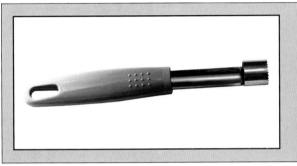

Apple corers

Have a rounded end to remove the core of an apple by pushing through the apple from top to bottom.

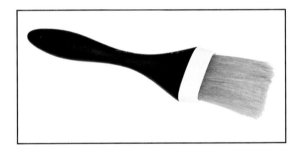

Basting brushes

Used to apply oils and marinades.

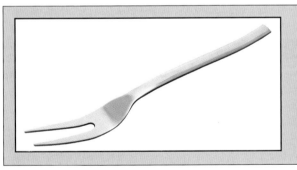

Carving forks

Have long pointed tines that hold meat securely in place while carving.

Cherry pitters

Hold individual cherries while pushing out the pits, also used for olives.

Citrus zesters

A small tool with a row of sharp holes at the end of its blade. Used to shred citrus peel.

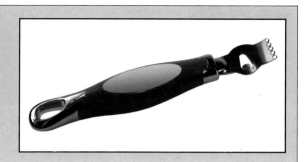

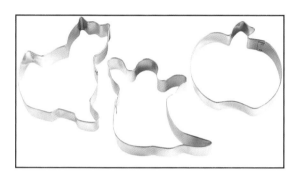

Cutters

Shapes made of stainless steel, copper, or tin used in baking.

Cutting or chopping boards

Made of wood or plastic in a variety of shapes and sizes to protect counters and knives when cutting.

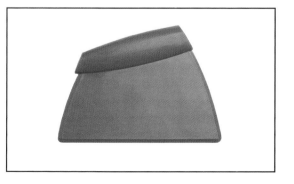

Dough scraper

A rectangular metal or plastic blade with a wooden handle along its top. Used to lift dough from a work surface.

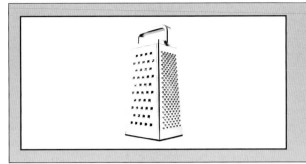

Graters
Usually made of stainless steel with sharp holes to assist in grating vegetables, cheese, fruit, or chocolate.

Herb mills
Have sharp covered blades for mincing fresh herbs.

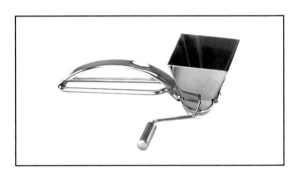

Instant-read thermometers
Are required by health boards to accurately measure temperatures to ensure proper food safety. The long tine can be inserted into meats or liquids.

Kitchen shears (scissors)
Used for general cutting tasks around the kitchen. Unlike regular scissors, the two sides separate to enable proper cleaning.

Kitchen twine

An all-purpose twine for tying stuffed or rolled meats, trussing poultry, or tying a bouquet garni.

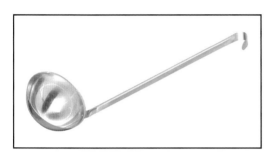

Ladles

Have long handles with a hook at the top and a semi-spherical cup used to lift liquids from stockpots.

Mallets

Usually made of wood or steel and are used for flattening meats and for cracking the hard shells of crustaceans.

Mandolines

Used to assist in slicing, shredding, or to julienne large quantities of vegetables. A variety of blades may be interchanged for different tasks.

Melon ballers

Semi-circular metal blades, round or oval, used to cut shapes from soft fruits and vegetables.

Mortar and pestle

An ancient tool used to grind and crush dried herbs and spices. They come in a variety of materials. The mortar is the bowl often having a rough inner surface and the pestle is a hand-held heavy pounder used to pound and crush the dried herbs against the mortar bowl.

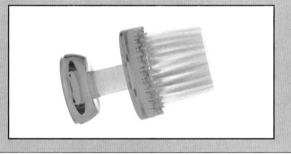

Mushroom brushes

Small hand held brushes with soft bristles used to remove dirt from delicate mushrooms.

Pastry bags and tips

Pastry bags are cone-shaped bags made of cloth or plastic and fitted with a variety of stainless steel or plastic tips. Icing, cream, filling or soft dough is placed in the bag and squeezed out of the top to form decorative patterns.

Potato mashers

Come in a variety of shapes, but usually have a metal wavy pattern on an extended handle. They are used to mash starchy vegetables after cooking.

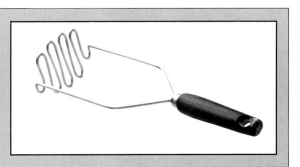

Potato nest fryer (bird's nest fryer)

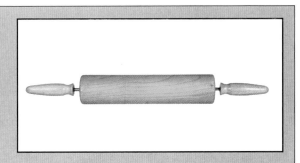

Ladle-shaped metal mesh spoons that clamp together. The bottom basket is filled with shredded root vegetables, usually potatoes, and then the other basket is pressed on top and clamped together. Next they are lowered into hot frying oil until the vegetable nests are crispy.

Rolling pins

Used for rolling dough and are often made of a long wooden cylinder with protruding handles at each end. Some models are without handles.

Sharpening steels

Have a long stainless rod, safety guard, and a handle. They are designed to provide an edge when a knife is run along the steel rod at a 20° angle.

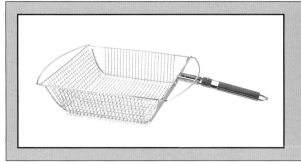

Sieves

Wire mesh straining baskets in varying degrees of fineness used for straining liquids. Some strainers are made to fit over pots and others have handles.

Sifters

Similar to strainers in that they have a mesh screen, but used for dry ingredients to strain lumps and impurities and for mixing dry ingredients together.

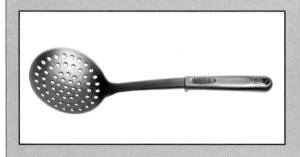

Skimmers

Similar in shape to soup ladles, but the ladle is flatter with holes or mesh. Used to strain impurities from the surface of stock and other simmering dishes. Also useful to retrieve items from a deep fryer.

Slotted spatulas

Same as other spatulas except for the slots, useful for removing foods cooked in fats.

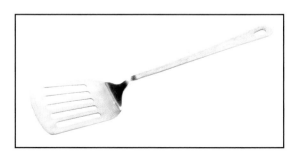

Spatulas

Made of metal, plastic, or rubber. Used for lifting foods from surfaces or for mixing or spreading soft substances.

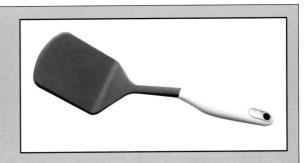

Strainers

Similar to sieves, but with a round bottom. Used for straining pasta, vegetables, and other foods.

Tongs

Long-handled tools used to pick up foods.

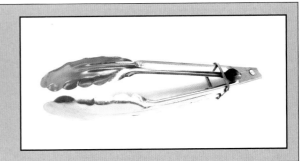

Whisks

Loops of stainless steel or plastic attached to a handle. Come in a variety of different types.

Wooden spoons

Popular stirring utensils for any kind of liquid, as they do not conduct heat and they stay cool in your hand.

Pots & Pans

Double boiler

A two-tiered pot where the lower section holds water and the higher section has a flat or perforated bottom in which to steam or cook food over indirect heat.

Sauté pan

There are many sizes and shapes of sauté pans. Sauté pans are usually shallow with sloping or straight sides and a long handle. These pans are used for cooking and frying in small quantities of oil.

Stockpot

Large high-sided pot with a lid and handles, used for soups, stocks, and stews.

Saucepan

Basic all-purpose pots with handles and high sides.

Sheet pan

A large, flat pan with short sides used in baking and often made of stainless steel or coated steel in assorted shapes and sizes.

Cast-iron skillet

A cast-iron skillet is a traditional heavy sauté pan used for frying foods. These skillets must be seasoned properly to prevent foods from sticking to the surface.

Baking pan

Similar to a sheet pan, but with a higher lip. Used for cakes and other baking.

Steam pan

Similar to a baking pan, but with a rolled lip. Varying shapes and sizes are used to insert into steam tables for holding foods at warm temperatures. They are also be called service pans, hotel pans, and counter pans.

Roasting pan

Roasting pans have deep sides, sometimes with a lid and usually with handles. It is usually made of heavy stainless steel. Roasting pans are used for roasting large pieces of meat and poultry.

Measuring Devices

Measuring cups

Used for measuring cooking ingredients. They are available in a variety of shapes, sizes, and materials.

Measuring spoons

Hold an exact amount of an ingredient when level.

Measuring cups

Made of assorted materials usually with a handle and pouring spout and with varying measurements labeled on the side of the cup. Used for both dry and liquid measurements.

Scales

A variety of scales are available that precisely measure the weight of food ingredients.

Larger Equipment

Open-element cook top

An open-element cook top uses gas or electric heating devices for cooking.

Hot top

A hot top is a flat steel-plated cooking surface under which burners heat the surface for searing foods.

Heavy-duty hot top

This is similar to other hot tops but designed for heavier weights.

Induction cook tops

Use magnetic energy transfer to heat specially designed pans. The surface is not hot to the touch, and the heat is instant when activated.

Conventional oven

This is a large box-shaped appliance with adjustable metal racks. The cavity is heated by gas or electricity to the desired temperature. Used for baking and roasting foods.

Convection oven

This appliance is similar to other ovens with the exception of having a fan that circulates hot air throughout the cavity. This promotes even and faster cooking, baking, and roasting.

Slow-cook ovens

These come in conventional or convection varieties, usually with a programmable thermostat enabling reduced temperatures for slow roasting or holding foods.

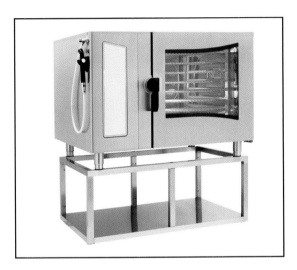

Combination steamer oven

This is similar to a convection oven, but with the option to add moisture to create steam cooking. Used for steaming vegetables or roasting foods that benefit from a combination of dry and moist cooking.

Barbecue ovens

Regular ovens where wood smoke can be produced to enhance the flavor of meats and fishes while baking or roasting.

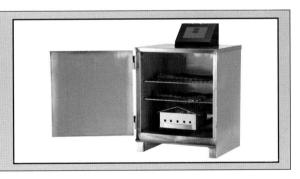

Microwave ovens

Use microwave radiation to heat food. Often used for defrosting, microwaves heat food from the inside out. This can be desirable in some circumstances.

Broilers and salamanders

Heating units where the heat source comes from above the platform for the food. Used to brown foods quickly as well as for cooking meats, poultry, and fish. The food platform can usually be raised or lowered to control the cooking process.

Grills

Heating units where the heat source is below the food platform. They are usually capable of very high temperatures and are effective for searing meats and seafood. The food platform usually consists of a heavy grill plate, which is designed to allow fat to drip down and away from the food.

Griddles

Flat heated surfaces that are usually used in breakfast production and sometimes for hamburgers. They must be cleaned and seasoned properly to prevent food from sticking.

Rotisseries

Rotating spits where meat is attached to the spit and rotated under the heat source. They can use gas or electricity.

Deep fryers

Fryers that hold liquid oil in a box-like well, which can be heated from underneath by gas or electricity. Fryers have a temperature gauge to control the temperature of the oil. Wire mesh baskets are usually used to lower food safely into the hot frying oil. At the base of the unit there is a valve that can be opened to drain the cooled oil when it needs to be replaced.

Pressure cookers

Used to cook food quickly with pressurized steam. These can be very dangerous so be sure to use caution.

Slicers

Used to cut cooked meat, cheese, and sometimes bread in a safe and uniform manner. A sharp blade rotates like a saw and the food is slowly guided past it into the catching tray. It is important to clean this machine properly after each use.

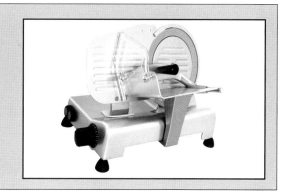

Steam tables

Used during service to hold foods at warm temperatures. A water well is heated by an electric coil. The steam pans, full of warm food, are placed over the steaming water to stay warm. A temperature gauge monitors the temperature of the water and a drain at the base of the well enables daily drainage. A tap valve is usually connected to a water supply to refill the well each day.

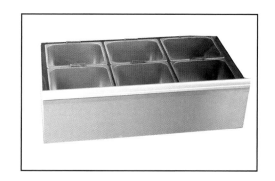

Cold tables

Refrigerated units that hold containers of food at a cold temperature during service.

Mixers

Motorized machines used to assist in mixing batters and dough at various speeds. Typically a mixing paddle can be lowered into a large bowl that rotates while the paddle mixes the contents in the bowl. Alternatively a whisk or beater attachment may be used.

Food cutters

Come in a variety of models and sizes and are used to chop large quantities of food items. Most cutters have assorted or interchangeable blades that will slice, dice, or shred.

Food processors

Motorized machines with cutting blades that roughly chop or, if processed longer, pureé ingredients. Assorted cutters and attachments can assist with varying tasks, from shredding and slicing to liquefying.

Steam kettles

Large cauldrons used to make soup and stock. They are mostly used in large production kitchens.

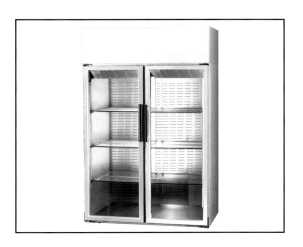

Refrigerator

A large appliance used to refrigerate foods in order to keep them fresh. Temperatures should be set below 5°C (41°F) and monitored regularly. Most fridges have adjustable shelves for storing different sized containers of food.

Freezers

Appliances designed to preserve food items for long periods by freezing them at temperatures below 0°C (32°F).

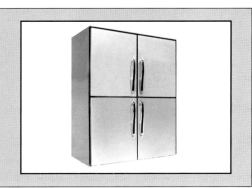

Chapter 6
Questions...

1. Name three tools that have been used for hundreds of years.

2. The tip of a knife is used for what kind of work?

3. How is a convection oven different from a conventional oven?

4. Name two useful tools for measuring.

5. True or **False:**

   A chef's most important tools are pots and pans.

▪ Chapter 7

Basic Cooking Methods

When cooking, one must make decisions as to the method of cooking to use in each situation. A variety of cooking methods are available in every kitchen, and each method has benefits that need to be considered. Your decision will depend on the ingredients you are working with, as well as the cooking equipment available to you at the time.

Dry and **moist** are the two major heat categories used in cooking. Moist heat cooking methods include boiling, blanching, braising, poaching, and steaming. Dry heat cooking methods include baking, broiling, deep frying, grilling, roasting, and sautéing.

Dry Heat Cooking Methods

Dry cooked foods usually have a crispy surface and are brown in appearance. This is because dry heat cooking causes the sugars in food to caramelize while cooking. The caramelizing process adds flavor, color and crispy texture. When cooking with dry heat, one wishes to avoid steam or moisture, as it will impede the caramelizing process. Therefore, always remove moisture from meats before you cook them. In addition, caramelize all food items before adding sauces or flavorings. Be sure to leave space between items when cooking as overcrowding items in a pan will also cause steaming. When cooking with dry heat always bring foods to room temperature before cooking to promote even cooking and caramelizing.

Grilling

Grills are heated by a variety of methods, including gas, electricity, and charcoal. The heat source is always below a grill rack on which the food is being cooked. Most grilling is done over very high heat for a short period of cooking time. The grill should always be preheated before you cook. To prevent sticking, it is advisable to rub some oil on the grilling surface. Be sure to dry food items completely before placing them on the grill. As you place the food on the grill, dark lines called grill marks will appear on the food. The food will release from the grill surface once it has caramelized. Cooks and chefs often turn the food two-thirds of the way through cooking each side. If you turn the food 45°, the grill marks will make a crisscross effect. Always remember to clean the grill with a wire bristle brush while it is still hot.

Griddles are a type of grill that is flat and sloped to allow the fat from food to roll down for collection. Lower temperatures are usually used for cooking items like pancakes or scrambled eggs.

Broiling

When broiling, food items are placed on an elevated slotted platform where a pan underneath catches the drippings from the food. The heat source is always above the food being cooked. High temperatures are often used and the cooking is controlled by moving the food items closer or away from the heat source. Always preheat the broiler before cooking. When broiling, leave the door open to allow any steam to escape from the cooking chamber. Use caution

when cooking fatty meats as the fat can flare up when too close to the heat source. Ideally the broiling rack should be 4 to 6 inches away from the heat. Broiling is often used as a finishing method to enhance the appearance of foods that have been cooked using other methods and would benefit from caramelizing.

Baking

Conventional and convection ovens are used for baking both sweet and savory dishes. Most baking is done at moderate temperatures between 300°F–400°F (149°C–204°C), and ovens should always be preheated before baking. Most baking requires some kind of vessel to hold the foods. Baking pans, muffin tins, and ramekins are all examples.

Cooking times for convection ovens should be reduced by approximately 10% because they cook food faster. If using a standard recipe, reduce the oven temperature by 25° and the cooking time by 10%. When cooking delicate egg dishes such as custards, bakers use a hot water bath called a bain-marie to protect the dishes from becoming too hot. The baking vessels are placed in a larger pan filled with water. This provides indirect heat. When using a bain-marie, always place the food dish and baking pans in the oven before adding the water.

Roasting

Roasting is similar to baking except that it uses fat as a cooking agent. As in baking, both conventional and convection ovens can be used. High-temperature roasting requires a preheated oven of 500°F (260°C), and low-temperature roasting, called slow roasting, is usually done at 250°F (121°C). Roasting is most often used with large cuts of meats or large amounts of vegetables. Roasting is also combined with pan searing in a two-stage method for cooking meats. Large cuts of meat are placed on a rack so that they do not sit in their own juices. As in other dry cooking methods, steam is kept to a minimum. Many large pieces of meat or poultry are started at a high roasting temperature for the first 20 minutes and then reduced to a slow roasting temperature for the remainder of the cooking time. When roasting vegetables, ensure even sized pieces to promote uniform cooking. Roast denser vegetables before lighter vegetables so that they are all done at the same time.

Sautéing

Sautéing is a cooking method where a small amount of cooking fat is heated in a pan over a stove top heat source.

Sautéing differs from deep frying in that the foods are not submerged in fat, just coated. Sautéing is a quick cooking method where foods are usually cut into small, thin pieces in order to cook quickly. Heat the pan, then the oil, before adding the foods to be cooked. This will prevent the foods from sticking to the pan. If the pan is smoking, then it is too hot and it is best to start again with fresh cooking fat. As in other dry cooking methods, foods should be dry before cooking to encourage good caramelizing. Many recipes call for breading items before cooking to create a crispy texture.

Pan frying is considered a form of sautéing, using additional fats in the pan and a longer cooking period. It is often a two-part cooking method where the items are finished in the oven.

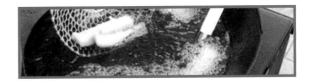

Deep Frying

Deep frying is a cooking method where the food is completely submerged in hot cooking fat. The cooking fat must be the correct temperature. If the correct temperature is used, food will be crispy on the outside and moist on the inside. If the temperature is too low, the cooking fat will be absorbed into the food creating a soggy and oily product. If the cooking fat is too hot, the food will burn on the outside while remaining uncooked in the center. Food items are cooked a few at a time to ensure an even temperature of the cooking fat. One must use great caution when deep frying as the hot fat can cause serious burns. Use a thermometer to maintain the correct temperature of the cooking fat. Proper frying temperatures are between 350°F (176°C) and 375°F (190°C). Always dry items before placing them in the fryer. NEVER PLACE ANY WATER OR WET ITEMS IN OR NEAR THE OIL, AS IT WILL CAUSE THE FOOD ITEMS TO SPATTER HOT COOKING FAT, WHICH CAN CAUSE SERIOUS BURNS. Cooking fat can take on flavors from the food that is cooked in it. Do not reuse oil that has been flavored by a previous food item. This could affect the quality of the new food to be cooked.

Moist Heat Cooking Methods

Moist heat cooking methods are preferred for achieving a moist and tender product. Food that is cooked by moist heat will not develop the caramelized crispy texture of dry cooked food. Moist heat cooking is most often done in a covered vessel in the oven or on the stove top.

Braising & Stewing

Braising and stewing are moist cooking methods where the food to be cooked is partially or completely covered in liquid while cooking. Stewing is a method where food is completely submerged in

the cooking liquid. Braising is a method of partially covering food in a flavorful liquid. These methods are often used in dishes containing meat, poultry, fish, and vegetables. Cooking liquids include wine, stock, water, and prepared sauces. Braised dishes usually include the cooking liquid as part of the dish. It is an ideal cooking method for less expensive and fatty meats that will benefit from a long and slow cooking process that will tenderize them. Meats are first seared, and then the cooking liquid is added. A long simmering period follows during which the cooking vessel is covered. A gentle simmer is desirable as rapid boiling can cause the meat fibers to toughen. When braising in the oven, a temperature of 325°F (163°C) is advisable. Monitor cooking liquids occasionally and if they become too thick, add water to the pot.

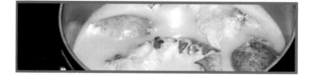

Poaching

Poaching is a moist cooking method used for shellfish, poultry, eggs, and meats. The food is cooked in hot liquid that is most often stock or water. Foods should be completely submerged in the hot cooking liquid and simmered gently until they are tender. Rapid boiling can cause protein fibers to toughen. The temperature of the liquid should remain between 160°F (71°C) and 180°F (82°C). The poaching liquid is usually brought to the boiling point before foods are added.

Steaming

Steaming is ideally suited for cooking fresh flavorful foods like vegetables and fish. Steaming describes very hot moist air. Specially designed ovens are used in large kitchens, and in small kitchens a rack is placed above boiling water. The cooking vessel is usually covered with a lid. Use great caution when cooking with steam as it can burn you very easily.

Boiling

Boiling is similar to poaching except that higher temperatures are used for the cooking liquid. As in poaching, foods are completely submerged in the cooking liquid. Boiling liquid is 212°F (100°C). Blanching is a method of dipping foods in boiling water for a couple of minutes. Green vegetables are cooked in boiling salted water. Root vegetables are started in cold water and brought to a boil then simmered until cooked through. Most boiling methods include simmering, where the liquid is 185°F (85°C) to 205°F (96°C). Simmering water produces small light bubbles, and boiling water produces active bubbles.

Other Methods of Cooking

Microwave cooking uses radiation heat transfer to cook foods from the inside out. Microwaves are mostly used in professional kitchens for warming prepared foods and for thawing foods. As microwave cooking can damage food textures, it is not widely used. Induction cooking is another form of heat transfer using magnets. It replaces electric elements in stove top cooking and heat sources in some ovens. It is not widely found in professional kitchens yet, due to its prohibitive expense.

These various cooking methods give you many options for cooking raw ingredients. Experience and experimentation will help you to understand the result of applying different cooking methods and how the varying methods will affect texture and flavor. With experience you will develop culinary judgment in deciding which method to use in each situation.

Chapter 7
Questions...

1. Name two types of heat used in various cooking methods.

2. Which of the following are dry heat methods of cooking?

   a. baking
   b. steaming
   c. roasting
   d. grilling

3. Which of the following statements are true?

   a. Larger cuts of meat are usually roasted on an elevated rack.
   b. Braised meats are usually browned first.
   c. Simmering water is bubbling rapidly.
   d. The heat source for broiling is above the food.

4. True or False:

   Pan-frying is exactly the same as sautéing.

5. At what temperature does water boil?

6. What happens to fried foods if the oil temperature is not hot enough?

7. True or False:

   Braised meats are always submerged in liquid.

Chapter 8

Mise en Place

Mise en place (say "*Mees on plas*") is a French term meaning to put in place. In culinary terms, mise en place is the process of preparing all necessary ingredients and organizing them in their proper place before you begin to cook. Cooking is a practice requiring precision and timing, and it is wise to prepare ingredients before the actual cooking process.

In professional kitchens, we do as much preparation ahead of time as possible. Some food items require peeling or chopping, others may require measuring, while other items may require blanching. Cooks and chefs are responsible for stations in the kitchen. Each station is assigned a list of tasks that must be completed before service. This list begins with the mise en place. This ensures that the station will run smoothly and efficiently at the time of service.

There are many things you can do to prepare for the cooking process. First look at the tasks you have been assigned. You will need certain equipment and tools to complete the tasks. If you determine what these are, and gather them up from around the kitchen, they will be readily available to you when you need them. Valuable time can be lost by searching for a needed item at a critical moment in the cooking process.

Next, look at the list of ingredients required to complete the tasks. Gather all the ingredients before you begin cooking. Once you have all of the ingredients, you can analyze to see what advance preparation is possible. Perhaps you could peel and chop carrots, measure cream, weigh flour, and have the ingredients ready in separate containers.

If you take the time to wash, trim, cut, and prepare your vegetables and meats, you will save valuable time in the cooking process. Most cooks and chefs use a variety of small containers to hold their recipe ingredients, tidily organized around their workstation. This practice helps them to keep organized and ready to cook in an efficient and timely manner. Always operating with this level of preparation will reduce mistakes, stress, and confusion in the kitchen.

Good practices for mise en place are important as often the majority of these tasks are assigned to cooks. The following are tasks you may be required to do to complete your mise en place:

- Washing vegetables, fruits, herbs, meats, fish, and shellfish
- Peeling vegetables and fruits
- Trimming and cutting vegetables, fruits, herbs, and meats
- Blanching vegetables, fruits, and nuts
- Breading vegetables, fish, and meats
- Marinating meats
- Pitting fruits
- Toasting nuts
- Weighing dry ingredients
- Measuring wet ingredients
- Preparing seasonings

Washing Fruits and Vegetables, Meats and Fish

It is critical to wash fruits and vegetables properly. There is nothing worse than learning that your customer found a slug in the salad or crunched on sand while eating vegetables. It may seem a tedious task, but if it is done properly, you will avoid catastrophe and embarrassment.

The first step is to make sure your hands and your work area, including the sink, are sanitized. Once you have insured a sanitary sink, fill it with cold water. Add some salt when washing leafy or green vegetables, as this will cause slugs and bugs to shrivel and float to the surface of the water. Remove the leaves and vegetables from of the water, and place them in a strainer over a bowl. Drain the dirty sink water and repeat this process until there is no dirt left on the surface of the water. Use your fingers to rub off any stubborn dirt particles.

Root vegetables such as carrots and potatoes may require a good scrub with a small brush or scouring pad.

Mushrooms can be cleaned with a small delicate mushroom brush. Mushrooms absorb water, so do not let them soak too long.

Fruit usually looks clean when it arrives from the supplier. Do not be fooled though, a good cleaning is still necessary. Be careful when cleaning berries, they are delicate and do not benefit from long soaking.

To wash meats and fish, rinse under cold running water and place in a colander. Pat dry with a clean cloth or paper towel. For sanitary reasons, do not reuse the towel after drying meats.

To wash shellfish and mussels, rinse them in a sink full of cold water. Lift out the shellfish and scrub off any dirt with a small brush. If there is a beard, as on a mussel, pull it off or use a paring knife to cut it off. Drain in a colander and refrigerate immediately.

Peeling Fruits and Vegetables

Many fruits and vegetables have tough outer skins. It is important to preserve the inner fruit as much as possible when removing the outer skin. Small paring knives and peeling tools are helpful for this task.

For root vegetables, trim off the ends and any eyes or rotten spots with your knife. Then use the peeler carefully to remove the skin.

Celery has tough veins that run through the stalk. If you snap the end without ripping entirely through, you can gently pull on the strands and they will lift out of the stalk. Alternatively, you may use a peeler to remove the outside layer containing the veins.

Thin skins are difficult to remove with a peeler or paring knife. Tomatoes, peaches, and apricots should be immersed in boiling water for 30 seconds. Once removed and cooled the skins will peel off easily. Be careful not to leave the items in the boiling water longer than 30 seconds or the flesh under the skin will start to cook and soften.

Citrus fruit has two layers of skin. Both layers need to be removed gently. The first layer is the colored skin used for zest, as it contains citrus oils and much flavor. The second layer is white pith, which clings to the fruit and needs to be removed entirely as it is

bitter in flavor. A paring knife is the best tool for this task. Cut across the top and bottom of the citrus. Place the citrus flat on one cut end, then slice between the fruit and the pith following the curve of the fruit from top to bottom. You can then section the citrus by cutting gently between each fruit segment and its membrane.

Melons have a tough outer skin. You can use a paring knife or chef's knife to cut off the top or bottom, then you can slice from the top to the bottom between the fruit and the tough outer skin. The seeds and membrane inside must be gently scooped out.

Pineapples have sharp, pointy leaves and a rough, thick skin. Use a sharp chef's knife to remove the first inch off the bottom of the fruit, then the first inch off the top of the fruit (plus the leafy top). Stand the fruit on a flat end and cut about 1/2 inch into the fruit from the top around to the bottom following the curve of the fruit. Small, hard bumps called eyes will remain. Use a small paring knife to gently carve them out. Next, remove the core of the pineapple, as it is very tough. Depending on the finished product you desire, you may then proceed to cut the pineapple into sections or rings.

Note: The sweetness of a pineapple is in the base. If you stand it on its leaves for a day or two before it is used, the sweetness will spread throughout the fruit.

Asparagus has a delicate fern-like top and stalks that become tough closer to the bottom. Rinse stalks well in cold salted water and then use a sharp knife to cut off any pale, tough ends. Next, use a vegetable peeler gently peel the bottom 2 inches of each stalk. Use a small paring knife to score the flat bottom of the stalks and stand them upright in a container with 2 inches of water.

To peel garlic cloves, remove the outer skin, then break apart the garlic into separate cloves. Using the flat side of a large knife, press down on the clove and the papery skin will break and release. Prepare the garlic as needed.

The thin skins of bell peppers are difficult to remove with a peeler. Scorch the skins by roasting the peppers in the oven or on a grill. The skin will then peel away easily from the flesh.

Pitting Fruits

Some fruits such as olives, cherries, and peaches have a hard nut-like pit (sometimes called a stone) in the middle. Most recipes require the removal of these pits. Small fruit like cherries and olives are easily pitted with a specially designed tool, called a cherry pitter. Alternatively, you can use a small paring knife to cut around the circumference of the fruit to open it. Next use the tip of the knife to pry the pit out gently. For larger fruit, use a paring knife to cut around the circumference of the fruit from top to bottom. Use your hands to twist the fruit halves in opposite directions. This will separate the fruit into two halves with one half containing the pit. To remove the pit, hold the fruit half in the palm of your hand, pit facing up. Take a knife in your free hand and stick the blade (not the point) into the pit. Use the embedded blade to help you twist out the pit. Do not use the tip of your knife to pry the stone out. If your knife slips, you may cut yourself. Use this method for avocados, plums, peaches, and nectarines. Some grapes contain small seeds called pips. To remove the pips from the grape, cut the grape in half and gently push out the pips. A good tool to use for this is the eye end of a trussing needle.

Blanching Vegetables

Blanching is a brief immersion in boiling water. It is done to partially cook vegetables in order to speed up the cooking process at the time of service. All green vegetables are dipped into boiling salted water for 1 to 2 minutes, then removed and placed directly into ice-cold water to stop the cooking process. To blanch root vegetables; place the vegetables into cold water, bring the pot to a boil, and then reduce to a simmer for 2 minutes. Remove the vegetables and run cold tap water over them to slow the cooking process.

Trimming Fruits and Vegetables, Meats and Fish

Trimming is usually done to remove any damaged flesh or to prepare the fruit or vegetable for presentation. Some examples of trimming are removing leaves from celery stalks, removing the stalks of fresh herbs, and trimming the pointy tips of a globe artichoke.

Similarly, with meats and fish, trimming is done to prepare the food for presentation. The chef will provide specific instructions for how the food should be trimmed. Generally, the fat around a cut of meat may need to be removed, or perhaps a piece of meat needs to be trimmed and/or tied to achieve a certain shape.

Cutting Fruits and Vegetables

There are several techniques for cutting vegetables into desired shapes and sizes. Basic terms are *slicing*, *dicing*, *chopping*, and *cutting*. Slicing is using your knife to make a controlled cut. Dicing is slicing in one direction and then another to produce a small cube shape. Chopping is a vigorous movement that is faster and less controlled. Cutting is a broad term to describe any of the above.

Professionals have names for these very specific shapes and sizes.

Dice Sizes for Fruit and Vegetables

- **Fine Brunoise**
  1/16" x 1/16" x 1/16" or
  1.5mm x 1.5mm x 1.5mm

- **Brunoise**
  1/8" x 1/8" x 1/8" or
  3mm x 3mm x 3mm

- **Small Dice**
  1/4" x 1/4" x 1/4" or
  6mm x 6mm x 6mm

- **Medium Dice**
  1/2" x 1/2" x 1/2" or
  12mm x 12mm x 12mm

- **Large Dice**
  3/4" x 3/4" x 3/4" or
  2cm x 2cm x 2cm

Slice Sizes

- **Fine Julienne**
  2" long x 1/16" x 1/16" or
  5cm x 1.5mm x 1.5mm

- **Julienne**
  2 1/2" x 1/8" x 1/8" or
  6cm x 3mm x 3mm

- **Batonnet**
  2.5 – 3" x 1/4" x 1/4" or
  6 – 7.5cm x 6mm x 6mm

Other Traditional Cut Shapes

- **Paysanne**

  (round, square or rectangular)
  1/2" x 1/2" x 1/8" or
  12mm x 12mm x 3mm

- **Rondelle**

  round or bias round (at a 45°
  angle) slices of various
  thickness and diameter

- **Tourne**

  (turned) 2" long x 3/4" in
  diameter with 7 sides and
  flat on the ends

- **Chiffonade**

  rolled leaves cut into fine
  shreds

Review the section on knives for proper technique. The more you practice, the easier and faster you will get at these jobs.

How to Marinate

Marinating is a practice used to tenderize and enhance the flavors of meat, game, and fish. Marinades contain acids naturally found in citrus juices or spirits, which soften meat fibers. Other ingredients in marinades add flavor. Many marinades are boiled first, but some marinades are uncooked.

For a boiled marinade, the ingredients are first brought to a boil and then left to cool before being poured over the meat. Ideally, the joint of meat you are marinating is fully covered by the marinade. If not, turn the meat frequently to get an even permeation. In some recipes, the marinade is added to the stock when cooking, or to the sauce served with the meat. With a boiled marinade (for meat with bones), let the meat stand in the marinade in the fridge for 24 hours. For game, marinate up to 3 days. With an uncooked marinade, allow fish, steak, and poultry to stand in the marinade 2 to 3 hours in the fridge before cooking.

Basic Beef Marinade

(for joint of meat about 2 1/2 pounds)

Ingredients

- 1 large onion, thinly sliced
- 1 large carrot, thinly sliced
- 1 stalk celery, thinly sliced
- 1 clove garlic, chopped
- 6 – 8 peppercorns
- 2 tbsp (30ml) olive oil
- 1 bouquet garni
- 2 cups (500ml) strong red wine

Method

- Cut the vegetables into thin strips
- Chop the garlic
- Add all vegetables to a pan with the other ingredients
- Cover and bring to a boil
- Reduce the heat and allow to simmer for 2 minutes
- Pour into clean bowl and let cool

Basic Marinade for Game, Venison, and Hare

Same as basic beef marinade, but add

- 2 tbsp (30ml) red wine vinegar
- 2 lemon rind peels
- 6 juniper berries (whole, dried)

Prepare as for the beef marinade. The addition of vinegar will help to tenderize tougher meat.

Basic Quick Marinade for Steak, Fish, and Poultry

Ingredients

- 1 tbsp (15g) onion, finely chopped
- 3 tbsp (45ml) olive oil
- 1 tsp (5ml) wine vinegar
- ground black pepper
- 3 tbsp (45ml) sherry

Method

- Place meat in a shallow dish
- Mix all ingredients and pour over the meat, fish, or poultry. Cover and refrigerate at least 2 hours
- Periodically turn the food in the marinade and spoon the marinade over the food to ensure even permeation

Before cooking, be sure to dry the marinade from the meat with a damp cloth or paper towel.

Breadings and Coatings

*Note: You can make your own breadcrumbs with a white sandwich loaf that is at least 2 days stale. Cut off the crusts and reserve. Break the bread into crumbs by pulsing in a food processor. Spread the crumbs on a sheet of baking paper and cover with another piece of paper. Leave in a dry warm place for a day or two. To make brown crumbs, bake the crusts in a low oven temperature (150°F/66°C) until golden brown, then pulse in a food processor until they reach the desired coarseness. Store in a sealed jar to prevent moisture.

Breading (Egging and Crumbing)

To make egging and crumbing easier and less messy, it is best to set up an assembly line.

- The first step on the assembly line is always flour, lightly seasoned with a pinch of salt and half as much pepper.
- Next, a couple of beaten eggs in a shallow bowl

- Then, on a large sheet of wax paper, the crumbs

You can then work from left to right until you have finished.

If breading a mixed food item, for example crab cakes or potato croquettes, you must first divide the mixture into even sized portions. Next, you must shape the portions as per your recipe on a floured board. Use palette knives to handle the items during the process. Lift the shaped items, roll in the flour, dip in the egg mixture, then lift them over and place them gently on the crumb sheet. Lift each corner of the paper to enable the crumbs to stick to all sides of your food item. Next lift the item to a clean plate sprinkled with a layer of crumbs and repeat with the remaining food items.

Now you have completed the preparation for the cooking stage (frying).

When preparing a fish fillet, after washing, use a paper towel to pat it completely dry. Roll the fillets in the flour, and shake gently to remove any surplus. Then draw through the egg mixture, first on one side, then the other, and hang over the egg mixture bowl to allow the excess to drip. Next, lay the fillets in the crumbs, and roll the paper and the fillet back and forth until covered with crumbs. Lift gently with a palette knife to a plate covered with a layer of crumbs.

There are three kinds of coatings:

Seasoned Flour with beaten eggs and dry white breadcrumbs

- Fish
- Cutlets
- Fritters

Fritter Batter

- Fillets of fish
- Sweet and savory fritters

Pastry

- Savory hors d'oeuvres
- Sweet desserts

Fritter Batters

There are many different kinds of fritters from different cultures. Common to most people is the batter used for fish and chips. Fruit fritters and batters for Asian vegetables are all derivatives. You can make the batter well in advance and keep it in the fridge. Add the egg whites just before frying.

Fritter Batter for Fish
Serves 8

Ingredients

- 1 1/4 cup (150g) all purpose flour
- 2 teaspoons (10g) dried yeast
- pinch of salt
- 1 2/3 cups (400ml) warm water
- 2 tbsp (30ml) vegetable oil

- 2 egg whites
- (optional) 2 teaspoons (10g) dried dill

Method

Sift flour, salt, and dill (if using) into a bowl. In another bowl mix the yeast with half of the warm water. Add the oil to the yeast mixture. Gradually add the flour mixture into the yeast mixture.

Add in the remaining warm water and stir until the mixture reaches the consistency of thick cream. Mix well until all ingredients have incorporated. Cover with cling wrap and leave in a warm place to rise, 15 to 20 minutes. Just prior to frying, whisk the egg whites to a stiff foam and fold into the batter

Fritter Batter for Fruit

(apples and bananas are most commonly used)

Serves 4

Ingredients
- 4 tbsp (60g) all purpose flour
- pinch of salt
- 2 egg yolks
- 1 tbsp (15ml) melted butter, or oil
- 1/2 cup (125ml) milk
- 1 egg white

Method

Sift the flour and salt into a bowl. Make a well in the center of the flour and add the egg yolks, melted butter, and milk. Gradually blend the wet ingredients into the flour until it becomes smooth. Rest the batter in the fridge for 30 minutes. Just before using the batter, whisk the egg white until stiff and fold gently into the batter.

Toasting Nuts

Toast nuts in the oven at a moderate temperature, and supervise until they start to turn a golden brown and you can smell their aroma. Remove and cool before adding to recipes.

Measuring and Weighing Ingredients and Seasonings

Before you start to cook, it is important to weigh and measure all required ingredients including seasonings. Keep them handy near your workstation, although some of your ingredients may need to be kept chilled at all times. The conversion charts on pages 154 to 157 can assist you when necessary.

Now that you have your mise en place in order, you are ready to start COOKING!

Chapter 8

Questions...

1. True or False:

   Mise en place means to get everything in place before you start to cook.

2. Which of the following are mise en place tasks?

   a. washing vegetables
   b. making soup
   c. toasting nuts
   d. baking cookies
   e. pitting cherries

3. What is the first step in washing vegetables?

4. Which of the following would benefit from blanching to remove their skins?

   a. nectarines
   b. grapes
   c. tomatoes
   d. apricots
   e. all of the above

5. What is the purpose of a marinade?

6. True or False?

   When egging and crumbing (breading), it is best to start with the crumbs.

7. What is the most common use for a fritter batter?

Chapter 9

Understanding Herbs, Spices, and Seasonings

Herbs, spices, and seasonings are essential for successful culinary dishes. They are used by chefs to create texture, color, heat, and other visual and taste sensations in food. It is important to understand the properties of each in order to enhance dishes in a pleasing way. Cooks and chefs add spices and seasonings to enhance and heighten the flavor of the main food ingredient of a dish. They should not be used to hide the flavor of an ingredient or rescue a poor tasting dish. The aim is to enhance, not to overpower the other flavors in the food.

Good quality fresh herbs are readily available at most supermarkets. An abundant variety of spices from around the world are available from markets and specialty stores. Dried and frozen herbs are also available. All herbs and spices are perishable, so it is advisable to keep only small quantities on hand and to buy fresh replacements as you need them.

Before adding herbs or spices, you should taste your dish and use your culinary judgment to make decisions as to how it could be enhanced. Herbs and spices should be added 30 minutes before the end of the cooking process. If cooked too long, their flavors will diminish. Add herbs and spices gradually while tasting to determine when you have reached the desired result.

Most seasonings are also best added 30 minutes before the end of cooking so as to allow them to cook along with the other ingredients, but not to cook too long, which diminishes the flavors. You should always taste your dish before deciding if and what herbs and spices you will add. Don't just toss them into your dish because the recipe calls for it. Use your own judgment and experience to evaluate what is necessary, then you can add a little at a time and taste as you go, stopping when you are satisfied. Adding too many spices is a mistake, as you can't go back once you have added too much.

We will give you some basics to build upon, but it is up to you to use your own judgment, and develop your own opinion.

The following is a list of herbs, spices, and seasonings commonly found in cooking:

Herbs

Basil
Bay leaves
Chives
Coriander leaf
  (cilantro)
Dill
Marjoram
Mint
Parsley
Rosemary
Sage
Tarragon
Thyme

Spices

Allspice
Caraway seed
Cardamom
Mustard seed
Chilies
Cinnamon
Cloves
Coriander seed
Cumin seed
Fennel seed
Fenugreek
Garlic
Ginger

Juniper berries
Mace
Mustard seed
Nutmeg
Paprika
Pepper
Saffron
Sesame seed
Turmeric
Vanilla

Other Seasonings

Salt
Sea salt
Lemon juice
Mustard
Liqueurs
Wine
Beer

There are many more herbs, seasonings, and spices in the world that are added to the list each year.

Herbs You Need to know

Herbs are the leaves of plants grown in temperate climates.

Basil

Bay Leaves

Basil

Basil is used often in Italian cooking and has a spicy aniseed overtone. Basil leaves are green or purple in color, with 150 varieties to choose from. Leaves can be rolled into thin slices called a chiffonade that can be used as a garnish for soups and salads. Gently tear the leaves to add to hot dishes. Use sparingly, as too much can overpower a dish.

Bay leaves

Bay leaves are used most often in their dried format as fresh leaves have a bitter flavor. They impart a spicy flavor similar to black pepper, but without the heat. Break or tear the dried leaves or add them whole to your cooking, but remove them from the dish before serving.

Fact: In ancient Greece, bay leaves were used to make laurel wreaths to crown the victors of battles or sporting events.

Chives

Chives are a member of the onion family and taste mildly of onion. They have a bright, fresh green color and are attractive in dishes. The flavor of chives complements many dishes containing poultry, egg, cheese, potatoes, and more. Fresh chives impart the best flavor and should be added just before serving. Freeze-dried chives are useful in soups and stews. Fresh chives is one of the four ingredients of the popular French herb mixture "Fines Herbes."

Coriander leaf (cilantro)

Coriander leaf comes from the same plant as coriander seed, but is very different in flavor. Coriander leaf imparts a pungent and earthy flavor to foods. Used in Asian and Latin American cooking, it complements tomatoes, chicken and fish dishes, and curries. The leaves are bright green when fresh, and they should not be overcooked as the flavor can overpower dishes if left in them for too long.

Dill

Dill is used widely as a garnish because of its attractive bright green and feathery leaves. It imparts a sweet aniseed flavor to foods and is a popular enhancement to fish dishes, especially salmon. Dill can also be used with poultry, dairy, eggs, cheese, soups, and pickles.

Fact: Dill has been used for medicinal purposes to treat colic, gas, and indigestion.

Chives

Coriander Leaf

Dill

Marjoram/Oregano

Mint

Marjoram/oregano

Marjoram/oregano is one of the herbs used in a Bouquet Garni. It is best known for use in Mediterranean dishes, as it is a good complement for lemon and olive oil. It can be used with poultry, meat dishes, pastas, pizza, cheese, eggs, and stuffing. It is mild with a sweet flavor. Most commonly used dried.

Mint

Mint is used in both sweet and savory dishes for its fresh, clean flavor. It has a strong green color and is used extensively as a garnish, whole or torn. Mint is often added to lamb dishes as well as veal, rabbit, peas, new potatoes, fresh fruit, and jelly. Dried mint will keep its color and flavor if stored properly in an airtight jar away from sunlight.

Parsley

Parsley is the most widely used herb. It complements most dishes and has a fresh mild flavor. It will not overpower delicate dishes, and it keeps its attractive green color. It is often used as a garnish. It is an essential ingredient in the bouquet garni, and the stems are often kept to add flavor to stocks.

Fact: Romans thought parsley necklaces would help them to avoid drunkenness.

Parsley

Rosemary

Rosemary is a small evergreen shrub with needle-like leaves that are used to flavor many dishes. The needles, if left whole are removed from dishes as they are tough. Finely chopped needles can be left in some dishes. It should be used sparingly as the strong bittersweet flavor will easily overpower other flavors. Rosemary is a great complement to lamb and pork, as well as oily fish, game, soups, vegetables, and tomato sauces. It helps to cut the richness of fatty foods and meats.

Rosemary

Sage

Tarragon

Thyme

Sage

Sage comes from an evergreen shrub with soft, fuzzy, pale green leaves. It has a medicinal pine-like flavor, which complements pork, veal, game, sausages, onion, cheese, stuffing, and poultry. It helps to cut the richness of fatty foods and meats.

Tarragon

Tarragon has long, slender, dark green leaves with a spicy strong aniseed flavor. It is used sparingly as it can easily overpower dishes. Popular for poultry, fish, veal, lamb, eggs, sauces, vinegar, and mayonnaise. If left cooking too long, bitterness will be imparted to the food. Tarragon is one of the four ingredients of Fines Herbes.

Thyme

Thyme is a popular perennial herb that has many varieties including lemon thyme and cardamom thyme. All are evergreen shrubs with small oval leaves. It is often used dried, and retains its color and flavor well. Thyme has a strong flavor and can cook in dishes longer than other herbs, but should be used sparingly. It enhances many dishes, especially Mediterranean dishes, fish dishes, pasta, poultry, and dishes containing lemon.

Spices You Need to know

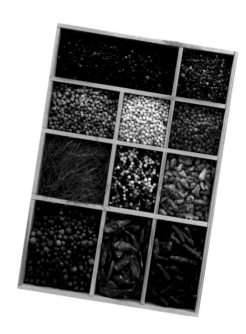

Spices come from the seeds, buds, roots, bark, and fruits of a variety of tropical plants and trees.

Allspice

Allspice, which comes from a plant in the Caribbean, is an unripe dried berry. It complements chicken, fish, sausages, pork, beef, cheese, pickles, fruitcakes, and cookies. Its name alludes to its flavor, which is a combination of cinnamon, cloves, and nutmeg.

Fact: The American Indians used allspice to flavor preserved meats.

Allspice

Caraway seed

Caraway seeds are small, uniform brown seeds with no stems. They have a mild aniseed flavor and add warmth to dishes. They are used to flavor rye bread as well as pickles, cheese, potato dishes, onion dishes, coleslaw, and cabbage.

Fact: It is thought that caraway aids the digestive process.

Caraway Seed

Cardamom

Chilies

Cardamom

Cardamom is pale green, plump pod filled with dark black seeds. The outer green pod is discarded and only the seeds are used, either whole or ground. The seeds are citrus-like with menthol undertones. The flavor complements curries, fish dishes, rice dishes, yogurt, pickles, fruit, and cream.

Fact: In many cultures cardamom is considered a powerful aphrodisiac.

Chilies

There are many varieties of chilies, all of which are pods of an annual plant. The membranes impart varying levels of spiciness to foods, ranging from mild to fiery hot. The longer the chilies remain in a dish the hotter the dish will become. Using whole chilies makes it easier to remove them at the end of the cooking process. Chilies are used extensively in Mexican, Indian, and South East Asian cooking. Avoid skin contact when preparing chilies by wearing rubber gloves, if possible. Touching or rubbing your eyes after preparing chili peppers will cause a painful burning sensation. Cayenne pepper is made from dried chilies and should be used sparingly.

Fact: Over 200 varieties of chilies are cultivated throughout the tropics.

Cinnamon

Cinnamon is made from the inner bark of a tropical evergreen tree. The bark is peeled, curled, and dried. When dried they resemble sticks that have a warm, sweet, woodsy aroma. When ground or broken, the oils are released and produce a stronger flavor. Sticks can be immersed in cooked foods and removed before serving. Cinnamon is often used in baking and complements chocolate, fruit, beef, pork, curry, pickles, and mulled wine.

Cinnamon

Cloves

Cloves are a very strong spice with a sweet and pungent flavor. They are the dried and unopened flower buds of a small evergreen tree. They are often mixed with other spices as in garam masala and Chinese five spice. Use in moderation as they can easily overpower dishes. Cloves are used extensively in Chinese and Indonesian dishes and complement apples, onions, ham, rice, desserts, and mulled wine.

Fact: Cloves are named after a nail, which they resemble. The word in French for nail is *clou*.

Cloves

Coriander Seed

Cumin Seed

Fennel Seed

Coriander seed

Coriander seed comes from the same plant as a cilantro leaf. The seeds are pale brown and dried, and they have a slightly pungent citrus flavor. They are used extensively in Indian cooking, especially in curries. The flavor complements pork, vegetables, cooked fruit, pickles, and chutney.

Fact: India is the largest producer of coriander seed.

Cumin seed

Cumin seeds are yellow/brown in color and are dried and usually ground before use. Cumin has a slightly bitter, earthy flavor. It is used in bread baking and complements cheese, rice, lentils, curry, chicken, and lamb. The seeds are often dry roasted immediately prior to using to enhance their flavor.

Fact: Cumin has been a taxable import to London since 1419 as it was a popular condiment in England.

Fennel seed

Fennel seed are small, oval, dried seeds that are light brown in color. They impart aniseed flavor. Fennel seed cuts the richness of fatty meats like pork and oily fish and complements potatoes, rice, cheese, eggs, apples, and pickles.

Fenugreek

Fenugreek is a strong flavored spice with a bitter curry flavor and is usually a main ingredient in curry powders. Also used in spice mixes such as Ethiopian Berbere and Sambhar Powder. Dishes spiced with ground fenugreek will take on a yellowish color. It complements curry, as well as pickles and chutneys.

Fenugreek

Garlic

Garlic is considered a spice when it is dried and ground. It has a different flavor from fresh garlic. Dried garlic is used in many savory dishes like soups, sauces, and marinades. It must be kept in an airtight container as it is prone to absorbing moisture.

Garlic

Ginger

Ginger is considered a spice when it is dried and ground. It has a sharp spicy flavor. It is often an ingredient in curry powders and is a complement to curries, fish, pickles, chutney, ham, and fruit.

Ginger

Juniper Berries

Mace

Mustard Seed

Juniper berries

Juniper berries are large, round purple berries that are the dried fruit of the juniper bush. They have a medicinal pine flavor and a peppery aftertaste. They are often used in game dishes, terrines, and other meat dishes and are a complement to cabbage.

Fact: A juniper berry takes 3 years to ripen on the bush.

Mace

Mace is a ground powder made from a lacey covering surrounding the hard shell of a nutmeg. The flavor is similar to nutmeg, but is milder in color and flavor. It is used in milk dishes such as béchamel sauce and whipped cream and complements puddings, cakes, cookies, potatoes, quiche, seafood, veal, and beef.

Mustard seed

Mustard seed is a strong and pungent spice that complements many dishes such as rabbit, veal, pork, fish, vegetables, cheese, and pickles. Mustard should only be added towards the end of the cooking process as it loses its pungency with heat.

Nutmeg

Nutmeg is the ground seed of a tropical tree. It has a sweet, warm, rich flavor and is used in milk-based desserts, sauces, quiche, cooked fruit, cakes, potatoes, vegetables, seafood, veal, and beef.

Nutmeg

Paprika

Paprika is a powder made from dried sweet peppers. It has a deep red color, and is often found in spice mixes like Baharat. It is mild and sweet with an earthy flavor.

Fact: Paprika is the national spice of Hungary. The conquering Turks introduced it to them in 1699.

Paprika

Pepper

Peppercorns are dried berries that come from a tropical vine. Black peppercorns are unripe green berries that become black and shriveled when dried in the sun. Green peppercorns are picked, dehydrated, then pickled whole. Removing the outer layer of ripe berries, drying the hard inner section, and grinding it into a powder makes white pepper. All pepper adds warmth to dishes and has a pungent, biting flavor. Pepper is widely used in any savory dish. Add pepper at the end of the cooking process as the flavor dissipates the longer it is cooked.

Pepper

Saffron

Sesame Seed

Turmeric

Saffron

Saffron is the yellow and orange stigmas of the autumn flowering crocus. They are dried and used sparingly as they are expensive. Saffron imparts a honey-like and mildly pungent flavor as well as adding a yellow-orange color to foods. It is often used in curries and complements rice, chicken, cakes, potatoes, yogurt, and cream.

Fact: Saffron is the world's most expensive spice. Most of the world's saffron is still hand picked and it takes more than 75,000 crocus flowers to produce a single pound.

Sesame seed

Sesame seeds are small, oval seeds from the fruit pod of a tropical tree. They are nutty in flavor and are often toasted or fried to enhance the flavor. Sesame seeds are often added to breads, salads, stir fries, and chicken dishes.

Turmeric

Turmeric is an earthy flavored ground spice, that has a rich, golden yellow color. It is most commonly found in Indian cooking in dishes like curry, rice, fish, chutney, pickles, eggs, and cream sauces.

Vanilla

Vanilla is a pod that comes from a variety of the orchid plant. The pods are picked while still green, and then cured to develop their flavor. Fresh vanilla pods are dark brown in color and pliable. The pods are sliced open to reveal hundreds of tiny black seeds, which are used to flavor custards, sauces, and creams.

Note: If you add herbs and spices or seasonings to cold and uncooked foods, it takes a few hours for the flavors to develop.

Other seasonings:
Salt

Salt is the most widely used seasoning in the world. Food is enhanced by the moderate addition of salt. Over-salting will ruin a dish; therefore, add salt gradually, tasting for the appropriate level. Professional chefs and cooks prefer to cook with sea salt for its subtle flavor. Most dishes will seem flat without the addition of salt.

Prepared mustards

Prepared mustards are used frequently to add flavor to sauces, dressings, and soups. They contain a mixture of mustard seeds, vinegar, and spices. Grainy European mustards, such as Dijon, are the most commonly used.

Vanilla

Salt

Prepared Mustard

Lemon Juice

Lemon Juice

Lemons are freshly squeezed for their juice, which is used both to cut the richness in foods as well as to lift the flavor of dressing and sauces.

Alcohol

Alcohol

Alcohol is frequently used in marinades and sauces as well as in braised and stewed dishes. Wine, liqueurs, and beer are all used to flavor dishes. In many dishes the alcohol content is burned off or evaporated so as not to be an element of the dish. Wine and beer have many different flavors to enhance foods. Experimentation will allow you to find your preferences. Strong wines, like Sherry or Madeira, should be added at the end of the cooking process. Liqueurs add their dominant flavor to a dish.

The following is a list of the dominant flavors present in various liqueurs:

Liqueur Name	Dominant Flavor
Amaretto	Almonds
Ananas	Pineapple and vanilla
Anisette	Aniseed
Aquavit	Caraway
Bailey's Irish Cream	Chocolate cream
Benedictine	Angelica
Cacao	Cocoa and vanilla
Café	Coffee
Calvados	Apples
Cassis	Black currants
Cerise	Cherries
Crème de Noyaux	Apricot and peach pits
Curacao	Orange and rum
Drambuie	Herbs, honey, and scotch
Framboise	Raspberries
Frangelico	Hazelnuts
Galliano	Herbs and vodka
Godiva	Chocolate
Grand Marnier	Oranges
Grenadine	Pomegranate
Kahlua	Coffee and vodka
Kirsch	Cherry
Menthe	Peppermint
Midori	Melons
Ouzo	Licorice, aniseed
Parfait Amour	Vanilla
Pernod	Anise and herbs
Sambuca	Licorice, aniseed
Tia Maria	Coffee and rum
Triple Sec	Oranges

Answer key p.180

Q Chapter 9
uestions...

1. True or False:

   Herbs and spices are added to foods to aid in visual and taste perception.

2. Herbs and spices _____.

   a. add interest to a dish
   b. create texture in a dish
   c. enhance natural flavors of the main ingredient in the dish
   d. all of the above

3. Spices can be used to mask the flavor of the main ingredient of a dish.

   a. Good idea
   b. Bad idea

4. When should you add herbs during the cooking process?

5. Name three herbs that are commonly used in cooking.

6. Why is saffron the world's most expensive spice?

7. What is the most widely used seasoning in cooking? Name two kinds.

8. Name three liqueurs you could add to give an aniseed flavor to a sauce.

9. If I add Kirsch to a cheese fondue, what flavor am I adding?

Chapter 10

The Recipe

What Is a Recipe?

On the road to becoming a professional cook, then a chef, there are many ways to learn your craft: from teachers, from experience, from textbooks, and from trial and error. Recipes are written guidelines for making culinary dishes. Every culinary dish can be made with many variations. Think of a Caesar salad: some recipes have anchovies and some do not. Some recipes have a creamy dressing, while others use a vinaigrette. There could be thousands of recipes for the same dish, each slightly different in some way. Recipes are used in professional kitchens to create standardized quantities and to ensure that the dish can be recreated in the same way each time. Otherwise, recipes are used as a guide to help you create dishes. You must also use your senses and your culinary judgment, and apply them to every situation. Then you can adapt recipes to your own liking and preferences.

Why Do Recipes Sometimes Not Work?

There are many reasons a recipe might not turn out the way we expect. Sometimes the instructions are unclear, or we interpret the writer's directions in a different way than intended. Variations in ingredients available or in specific details can alter the outcome of the recipe. Other influences such as weather can also affect the outcome of a recipe. If a kitchen is too cold, bread may not rise. If a kitchen is too humid, meringues could collapse. We must use our judgment to the best of our ability, knowing that even in doing so, sometimes things just do not work out.

Good recipes are clear and have a precise list of ingredients with simple directions to follow for the cooking method. A photograph showing a good example of the finished product can be very helpful.

Typically the first section of a recipe contains a list of ingredients, including the quantity required for each. The quantities vary from vague descriptions (a pinch of salt), to very precise descriptions (34ml of freshly squeezed lemon juice). They can also be described in terms of a count (5 ripe plum tomatoes), a measure by weight (pounds, grams), volume (cups, tablespoons), or a visual portion (1 slice of bread).

A variety of weights and measures are used, incorporating both traditional and modern measuring methods. Sometimes a recipe will use one or the other, or both at the same time. It is a confusing system, but you must learn both as you will come across all of these measurements in professional kitchens. Keeping a table of equivalency handy (one is provided at the back of this book) will help you to convert the measures when necessary. Measuring calculators can assist you in doing calculations as well.

How to Measure Ingredients by Weight

Kitchen scales come in many varieties, and they are readily available and inexpensive. Some are more precise than others. Most chefs use an electronic scale with a digital readout.

How to Measure Liquids

Liquid ingredients are most often measured by volume. Measuring cups are commonly used and have markers on the side with varying volumes. You use the markers as a guide for how high to fill the cup. Be sure to measure ingredients on a level surface to ensure accuracy. Liquids can also be measured by weight in the same manner as other ingredients. An equivalency chart for weight and volume is provided at the back of the textbook.

Methods for Cooking

The second section of most recipes is the description of the procedures and methods for cooking. These can be organized in different ways: some divide tasks into a time table (three days ahead, two days ahead, same day), others divide tasks into categories such as preparation, cooking, or storing. All should clearly outline instructions for fulfilling the recipe in a concise and easy-to-follow manner. Most recipes use a point form for instructions and follow a timeline for preparation, explaining what task to do first and continuing in sequence of necessary actions, including the length of time required to accomplish each task. Many recipes include other helpful information, advice, and nutritional information. Professional recipes usually contain the quantity of product the recipe makes, the portion size, and the number of portions per recipe. This aids the chef in planning quantities or deciding to adapt the recipe by converting the amounts of ingredients to make more or less. It is advisable to use recipes that are meant for the quantity you need as some recipes do not work when adapted.

In converting recipes, multiply each ingredient by the amount you wish to increase or decrease the recipe by. The cooking time often does not change significantly, so it is advisable to monitor the item while cooking until the desired results are achieved.

Sample recipe conversion:

A chef wants to double a recipe for four portions to make enough for eight portions.

Multiply by 2		
(4 Servings)		(8 Servings)
2 cups	x 2	4 cups
300g	x 2	600g
4lbs	x 2	8lbs

When converting recipes, take care with herbs, spices, and seasonings. Add them gradually while tasting the dish until you achieve the desired results.

Photos can be very helpful to assist in visualizing the desired outcome. Use them only as a guide, and remember to add your own creative flair to the finished presentation. In some cases, you may be required to present a dish that is identical to the photo.

Remember that when producing colorful recipe books, many tricks of the trade are used to make the photographs look enticing. Food stylists sometimes use fake products in the photographs, so use your own judgment. If your outcome is slightly different from the photo, but you think it looks, smells, and tastes good, than likely nothing is wrong. If your outcome looks vastly different from the photo provided, and you think it looks bad and tastes awful, than either mistakes were made interpreting the recipe or other factors were involved. Don't worry, every cook and chef has a multitude of funny stories from situations where things went wrong. Add one to your repertoire, and try another recipe!

Chapter 10

Questions...

1. True or **False:**

   There is only one recipe for each dish in the world.

2. Which of these are acceptable measures of ingredients?

   a. a dash of lemon juice
   b. 2 whole apples, peeled
   c. 25 grams of flour
   d. one scoop of ice cream
   e. all of the above

3. Name two reasons why a recipe might not work.

4. True or **False:**

   When you double a recipe, the cooking time doubles as well.

5. Name two methods of measuring an ingredient.

6. True or False:

   You should not expect that a product you make will look exactly like the photo in a cookbook.

Chapter 11

Stocks

What Are Stocks?

Stocks are found in most professional kitchens and are the basis upon which soups and sauces are made. Stocks are not eaten in their original form, but as an element of other dishes. Stocks add a depth of flavor to dishes since they concentrate liquids extracted from vegetables, meat, or fish, and seasonings.

Making stock is a labor-intensive process that requires time. However, it is time well invested as the impact on the overall taste of your food is invaluable. Processed substitutions are available in the form of liquid and powder, and they are used widely as a time-saving shortcut. If used properly they can produce acceptable dishes; however, the resulting flavor is never as good as the real thing. It is wise to make large quantities of stock and store it in your freezer. You will benefit from the extra time spent, by the compliments and praise you will receive for your flavorful dishes. Many of the substitute bases are extremely high in sodium and can taste very salty if too concentrated. Be careful to taste and season accordingly. Real stock, it can be argued, is a better product for both health and quality.

In a professional kitchen, stocks are often made in large quantities.

Leftover fish bones and meat bones are stockpiled and frozen until enough are available to make a large quantity of stock. This is an efficient use of products that would otherwise be thrown in the garbage.

It is important however, not to put "garbage" in the stock. There is a difference between using up produce and using produce that should be in the garbage. If you use rotting vegetables in your stock, your stock will taste like rotting vegetables. Use only good quality products before they become spoiled. Chefs use two terms to talk about the subject of using supplies wisely. The first is, "garbage in, garbage out!" which means that if you put garbage into your dish that is what you will get, garbage! The second saying is "FIFO," short for "first in, first out." This is a description for the practice of using up products that have been stored in the fridge the longest before using or opening a newer product. As produce and supplies are delivered, the cooks and kitchen helpers are told to place the newest products at the back of the fridge and move forward the older products. This practice may seem an effort in organization, but wasting products out of laziness adds to excessive food costs and can cause a loss in profits.

It is not always possible to make stocks from leftovers. Many suppliers can deliver boxes of bones or fish scale when necessary. There are many different kinds of stock. We will learn those most commonly used and how to make them in both small and large quantities.

The following stocks are found in today's professional kitchens:

Commonly Found

- Vegetable stock
- Chicken stock
- White stock (Veal and beef bones)
- Brown stock (Veal and beef bones)
- Fish stock

Specialty Stocks (rarely found)

- Lamb stock
- Shellfish stock
- Game stock
- Ham stock
- Turkey stock

We will start with vegetable stock. This stock is being used more and more, as there exists a need to satisfy the increase in demand for vegetarian dishes in the market place. In the past, many chefs commonly added chicken stock to soups and sauces for extra flavor. Now, vegetable stock is more common because you are able to sell the item to a wider market of diners.

What Is a Bouquet Garni?

A **bouquet garni** is a small bundle of herbs and seasonings used to add flavor to hot liquids. The bundle is usually encased in leek leaves and tied with kitchen twine. Once prepared it is dropped into the stock or soup as it simmers to release flavors into the stock. The other end of the string is tied to the handle of the stock pot so it can be removed at the end of the simmering process.

Traditionally a bouquet garni will contain an assortment of fresh light herbs such as parsley and thyme; light vegetables such as celery and leeks; and seasonings such as peppercorns, cloves, or juniper berries.

To Make a Bouquet Garni:

- Place a 5-inch (12.5cm) stretch of the outer layer of a leek on your work surface

- Place some peppercorns or other seasonings on the leek

- Place fresh herbs and vegetables on the leek

- Use the leek to wrap the bundle keeping all contents together and tie it tightly with kitchen twine. Leave a long tail of string so you can tie it to the pot handle when you use it

- If you don't have a leek, a piece of cheese cloth can also be used to tie the bundle. A bundle tied with cheesecloth is called a **sachet**.

What Is a Bain-Marie?

A **bain-marie** is a water bath. It is used in many different applications to control the temperature of an ingredient. Sometimes you will place a bowl with a warm liquid in it over a larger bowl filled with ice or cold water. This will help to chill the liquid in the upper bowl. For larger pots of liquid, the sink can be used in the same manner. If you place a baking rack at the bottom of the sink to elevate a pot of warm liquid and run the cold water tap to surround the base of the pot, this will help to chill it.

Some sinks have a removable overflow drainpipe, which when inserted into the drain allows the sink to fill up to the height of the pipe. This allows you to fill the sink higher while still running the tap water without overflowing the sink. Stir the liquid in the pot to assist in chilling faster. Another use for a water bath is to protect delicate items while cooking in the oven. In this case a large cooking vessel such as a baking pan is filled with water to surround smaller baking vessels filled with the item to be cooked. The water bath keeps the items being baked from heating too quickly, which causes separation or burning.

Vegetable Stock

Makes about 3 to 4 quarts (4 liters).

Ingredients

- 2 tsp (10ml) olive oil or other oil
- 3/4 cup (150g) chopped onion
- 3/4 cup (150g) sliced leeks
- 6 quarts (5 liters) cold water
- 1 cup (200g) chopped carrot
- 1/2 cup (100g) chopped celery
- 1 cup (200g) quartered mushrooms, any kind
- 1 bouquet garni

Method

- In a deep-sided sauté pan, sweat (cook) the onion and leeks in the oil, over low heat for about 6 to 8 minutes.

- Add remaining vegetables, water, and bouquet garni (tie the bouquet garni string to the pot handle so you can easily remove it).

- Bring to a boil, then reduce to a gentle simmer for 30 to 45 minutes.

- Strain through a fine chinois strainer into a clean pot. Cool in a bain-marie.

Note: Sweating is cooking slowly over low heat. This allows the natural sugars in onions and similar vegetables to cook and sweeten without burning. When they brown, the natural sugars in the onions, garlic, or leeks are caramelizing. Caramel is cooked sugar. Sometimes caramelizing is the objective, but when making a white stock, we want to make a light and clear stock, and we don't want to caramelize the meat or vegetables. When we want a dark stock, the caramelizing process adds the deep rich color and flavor to the stock.

If you brown all of the vegetables first, you will produce a dark stock, which is a good substitute for beef stock in French onion soup or other recipes where brown stock is used. This is becoming more common to accommodate vegetarian diners.

To brown the vegetables, roast them all together in a 380°F (193°C) oven for 45 to 60 minutes until brown.

Remove to smaller containers to keep in the fridge for 3 days or in the freezer for 3 months.

Chicken Stock

Ingredients
- 1 1/2 lbs (675g) chicken carcass pieces
- 1 chopped onion
- 1 chopped carrot
- 1 chopped celery stalk
- peppercorns
- 1 bouquet garni
- 4 quarts (3.75L) cold water

Method
- Place all of the ingredients in a deep sauté pan.
- Bring to a boil, then reduce to a simmer. Let simmer for 2 to 3 hours.

- As the scum rises to the surface, skim it off with a large spoon. Continue to skim occasionally while the pot simmers.

- Strain the stock through a fine mesh strainer into a clean bowl. Allow to cool in a water bath, and place in the fridge.

- Chill the stock overnight until it solidifies. A thick layer of hard fat will cover the surface of the liquid, which should be jelly-like (see note below).

- Remove and discard the fat layer.

- Rewarm to a liquid, and place in clean containers in the fridge where it will keep 2 to 3 days or in the freezer where it will keep for 3 to 4 months.

Note: When a stock is chilled, it develops a jelly-like consistency. Why? There is gelatin in the bones that is released into the liquid as you cook them. When the liquid cools, the gel hardens. Cartilage is the source of the most gelatin. Knuckle bones, necks, feet, and shank bones contain greater quantities of gelatin and are often used for stocks.

If you don't have time to chill the stock overnight, you can remove the layer of fat from the surface of the stock using several paper towels. Gently place a paper towel over the surface of the stock for a few seconds, then remove and discard. Repeat this a few times until the layer of fat is removed.

Note: Never place a container of hot liquid directly into the fridge or freezer. The heat and steam will place pressure on the motor to keep the fridge/freezer chilled and could contribute to or cause motor failure. This could also damage other perishable foods that are located in the fridge/freezer. It is a better practice to chill liquids in a bain-marie, which will cool the liquid quickly.

White Stock

Recipe: Stock is made with the amount of veal or beef bones available and a rough recipe method is used for estimating the amount of ingredients.

Take the amount of bones, add 10% of the quantity of bones in vegetable mirepoix (onions, carrots, and celery), add one bouquet garni and cover the whole amount in water, approximately double the quantity of bones.

This is the way it is done in the kitchen. This is not precise as it is an exercise in using what you have. However, the method must be followed to produce a good quality stock.

First blanch the bones to remove any blood, fat, and protein.

Note: Bones should be no longer than 4-inch pieces. If necessary, cut/saw the bones into smaller pieces.

To blanch the bones, thaw and rinse the bones in cold water.

- Place the bones in a large soup pot and fully cover with water (about double the quantity of bones)

- Bring to a boil

- Scum will float to the surface of the pot. With a large spoon, skim the scum off the surface and discard it. Continue this process for a few minutes until most of the scum is removed.

- Drain the bones and rinse again under cold water

- Place the blanched bones in a large stock pot and cover with cold water

- Bring to a boil, and then reduce to a simmering boil

- The scum will rise to the surface. Skim it off with a large spoon and discard.

- Add the chopped vegetable mirepoix, and the bouquet garni. Tie the string to the pot handle.

- Continue to let the stock simmer, and skim the surface as necessary. Do not let the stock boil rapidly; this will cloud your stock as the scum will mix back into the stock.

- If the water level falls below the bones, add more water. The bones must be submerged so the scum can rise up to the surface of the stock for removal.

- Simmer and skim for 6 to 8 hours.

- Strain the stock through a fine-mesh Chinois strainer into a clean pot. To create a really fine mesh, line the strainer with one or two layers of cheesecloth.

- Cool the stock by placing the pot on blocks in the sink and running cold water around it. Stir until cool.

- Place in smaller containers in the fridge (will keep 2 to 3 days), or the freezer (will keep for 3 to 4 months).

Note: If you put the cooled stock in many small containers, then you are able to thaw just the amount you need each time you have a project requiring stock. At home, use an ice cube tray to freeze the stock, and then transfer to a freezer bag. When making a sauce or soup, you will have ready a small amount to defrost in the microwave or in a saucepan to make your soup or sauce sensational! If you clean milk cartons thoroughly, you can freeze stock in the cartons. Once frozen, remove the milk container and put the block of stock in a freezer bag. You can then stack the blocks for future use. If you are not going to freeze your stock, you can keep it in the fridge, but you must boil it every third day. When you remove it from the fridge, remove any fat from the top. Bring to a boil for a few minutes, then cool in a water bath. Return to the fridge for another few days.

To make a large batch of chicken stock:

Follow the instructions for white stock, substituting chicken bones for veal/beef bones, and simmer the stock for only 3 to 4 hours.

To make a large batch of fish stock:

Follow the same method as for white stock, using white fish carcasses (no eyes or gills) instead of beef/veal bones.

It is difficult to make clear stock from fatty fish such as salmon. Choose white fish for a good quality stock. It is not necessary to blanch the fish bones first. Simmer the fish stock for only 30 to 45 minutes.

Fish Stock

Recipe for making a small quantity of Fish Stock:

Ingredients

- 4–5 lbs (2kg) fish bones (no eyes or gills)
- 3 quarts (2 3/4L) cold water
- 12 peppercorns
- 1 bay leaf
- 1 celery stalk, chopped
- 1 onion, chopped
- 1 tbsp (15ml) salt
- juice of one lemon

Method

- In a large bowl, soak the fish bones in cold water and the salt for 10 minutes.
- Drain and rinse the bones in cold water.

- Place the bones in a deep sauté pan with the cold water, peppercorns, bay leaf, celery, onion, and lemon juice

- Bring to a boil, then reduce to a simmering boil

- Simmer 20 minutes while skimming any scum off the surface of the stock

- Strain the stock through a fine-mesh strainer into a clean container

- Cool in a water bath, and refrigerate for 2 to 3 days, or freeze for 3 to 4 months

Brown Stock

Makes 3 gallons (10 to 12 liters)

Ingredients

- 16 1/2 lbs (7–8 kg) veal or beef bones (4-inch pieces or smaller)

- 4 gallons (15L) cold water

- 1 1/2 lbs (750g) chopped onion

- 3/4 lb (375g) chopped carrot

- 3/4 lb (375g) chopped celery

- 1 1/2 lbs (750g) tomato paste or purée

- 1 bouquet garni

Note: When making brown stock, do not blanch the bones.

Method

- Place the bones in a deep roasting pan and coat very lightly in oil

- Roast at 400°F (204°C) for 1 hour and 15 minutes, until the bones are browned

- Remove from the roasting pan and place in a large stock pot

- Cover the bones with water

- Bring to a boil, then reduce to a simmering boil

- Tie the bouquet garni string to the pot handle and drop it in

- Use the roasting pan from the bones and add the vegetable mirepoix (onions, carrots, and celery)

- Roast the mirepoix for 10 to 20 minutes until browned and caramelized

- Add the browned mirepoix to the stock pot

- Skim the surface of the stock as necessary

- Add water to the roasting pan to deglaze (release the flavors stuck on the pan)

- Add this liquid to the stock pot

- Add the tomato purée or paste to the stock

- Simmer and skim for 8 hours

- Strain through a fine Chinois strainer into a clean pot

- Cool in a water bath in the sink on blocks

- Transfer to clean containers for storage in the fridge (2 to 3 days) or freezer (3 to 4 months).

Recipe for making a small quantity of Brown Stock
Makes 3 to 4 quarts (3.5L)

Ingredients
- 4–5 lbs (2kg) beef/veal bones
- 1/2 small onion, chopped
- 2 carrots, chopped
- 1 leek, chopped
- 1 celery stalk, chopped
- 5 quarts (4L) cold water
- 3 tbsp (45ml) tomato paste or purée
- 1 bouquet garni
- 6 peppercorns

Method
- Place all ingredients in a roasting pan coated in very little oil
- Roast in a hot oven 400° F (204°C) 1 hour till browned
- Remove to a deep sauté pan or soup pot
- Cover with cold water
- Add tomato paste, peppercorns, and bouquet garni
- Bring to a boil, then reduce to a simmer
- Simmer for 4 hours, skimming the the surface frequently
- Strain through a fine-mesh strainer into a clean container
- Cool and refrigerate until jellified and the layer of fat can be removed from the top
- Rewarm to liquid form to place in small containers to keep in the fridge (2 to 3 days) or the freezer (3 to 4 months).

*Notes:

- Do not overcook your stock. It used to be a common practice to let your stock boil away all day. It has now been proven that stock is at its best after the cooking times provided above. If you continue to cook the stock, you start to lose optimum flavor.

- Achieving clarity is of great importance. Never let the stock boil rapidly, keep it at a simmer. Skim frequently to remove as many impurities as possible. Use a fine strainer when straining. If your strainer isn't fine enough, use several layers of cheesecloth in your strainer to create a finer mesh to strain through.

- Never add starchy vegetables to your stocks. They will make it cloudy.

- Never use dark green vegetables like spinach or broccoli. They are too strong and will overpower the other flavors in a stock.

- Never use beets in a stock, they will turn your stock red!

- Salt is never added to stocks. Stocks are often reduced greatly and become very concentrated. If salt is added to the stock, it might end up too salty. It is best to save the addition of salt until the sauce is prepared. Then you can taste it and decide how much seasoning you think is necessary.

- White wine is occasionally added to stocks, most often to fish stocks, for added flavor.

What Is Broth?

Broth is similar to stock in that it is a liquid flavored by meat, fish, and vegetables. Stocks are primarily made from the bones and skeletons of fish and meats. Unlike stock, broth is made from cooking whole or large pieces of meat, poultry, or fish. Broth is the byproduct of cooking these items and using the flavored liquids from the cooking process. It is not as refined as stock in its clarity or flavor. It does, however, serve a similar purpose in that it adds flavor to dishes. For example, if you poach a chicken, when finished poaching the poaching liquid would be infused with chicken flavor. This is a broth.

What Is a Reduction?

We sometimes boil a stock to reduce it in quantity. Essentially, we are evaporating the water content of the stock, and concentrating its flavor. We do this for several reasons.

We may want to add flavor to a dish without changing its consistency, or we might want to store this flavor enhancer in a smaller quantity to save space in the freezer. Water can always be added back into it at a later date. We may only want to reduce it a bit to adjust the flavor, because it was not concentrated enough.

What Is a Glaze?

A glaze is a stock that has been reduced until there is very little water content remaining. It becomes a thick and syrupy concoction that is very concentrated in flavor. A small amount of glaze will add a lot of flavor to a dish. It can also be brushed onto a meat to enhance flavor.

Traditionally, there are three kinds of glaze:

Glace de Viande
"glass duh vee awned"

- made from brown stock

Glace de Volaille
"glass duh vawl oy"

- made from chicken stock

Glace de Poisson
"glass duh pwa sohn"

- made from fish stock

To reduce a stock to a glaze:

- Bring the stock to a boil, then reduce to a simmer.

- Skim away any impurities while continuing to simmer until it reduces to a sticky, thick syrup.

- Cool and place in an airtight container to keep 2 to 3 weeks in the fridge.

There are a few very good manufactured glazes available in the marketplace, made traditionally and quite decent in quality. Beware, the salt content can be strong.

Chapter 11
Questions...

1. True or **False:**

   Stocks are served at expensive restaurants.

2. Name three commonly found stocks in the kitchen.

3. Which of the following ingredients may be found in a bouquet garni?

   a. peppercorns
   b. thyme sprigs
   c. celery
   d. leeks
   e. parsley sprigs
   f. all of the above

4. Why is kitchen twine attached to a bouquet garni?

5. A bain-marie is used to _____.

   a. protect delicate egg dishes
   b. help to cool a liquid in a pot
   c. add liquid to a soup

6. What are the three traditional glazes, and what are they made from?

CHAPTER 12

Sauces

It can be said that the mark of great chefs lies in their ability to create exceptional sauces. If they are exceptional, sauces are a component for which a chef can become famous. A sauce is often the most interesting part of a creative dish. Its purpose is to enhance the presentation and taste of the feature food on the plate. Most cooks and chefs strongly feel that it is important to learn proper techniques for sauce making. Once the basic techniques are mastered, infinite variations can be produced that allow the chef to express creativity.

A sauce is added to a dish to enhance the flavor of the accompanying food item. It can enhance in two ways. The first is "taste perception." A sauce can impart a perception in the mouth as in richness, lightness, warmth, tang, and moisture. The second enhancement is "visual perception." Adding color and visual interest to a dish can help to please the diner. In order for these two enhancements to take place, a chef must create balance in the sauce. A sauce should not have any overpowering sensations. Its flavors should be either a complementary enhancement or a contrasting enhancement to the taste of the feature food item. The sauce must be seasoned properly. Too little or too much seasoning may ruin the sauce. The expected consistency of a good sauce is smooth, not lumpy or starchy, and thick enough to stay on the food without seeming gluey. A good sauce has a pleasing color and texture and improves the dish it enhances.

How to Make Sauces

There are six base sauces in traditional sauce making. All other sauces are variations of these base sauces. Base sauces are sometimes called leading sauces, or mother sauces. Most base sauces are not palatable on their own. All require additions of flavors and seasonings to make them taste good. As we learn each base sauce we will look at how the base sauce is used to create a variety of other sauces (called small or secondary sauces).

There are six base sauces:

Béchamel
  say "beh sha mel"

Velouté
  say "ve lou tay"

Espagnole
  say "es pan niol"
  (also called brown sauce)

Tomato sauce

Hollandaise sauce
  say "holl on days"

Fond lie
  say "phon de leeay"

All of the base sauces are made with one of these five liquids:

- Milk
- White stock
- Brown stock
- Tomato purée (with added stock)
- Clarified butter

These five liquid ingredients are then thickened with one of these five thickening agents:

- White roux
- Blond roux
- Brown roux
- Cornstarch
- Egg yolks

Incorporating a liquid and a thickener makes each of the base sauces:

Béchamel
  = milk + white roux

Velouté
  = white stock + blond roux

Espagnol
  = brown stock + brown roux

Tomato sauce
  = tomato purée/stock + optional roux

Hollandaise
  = clarified butter + egg yolks

Fond lie
  = brown stock + cornstarch

Roux

A **roux** is an equal combination of flour and fat that has been cooked together. Professional kitchens usually use all purpose or bread flour. Cake and pastry flour can be used, but will not thicken a sauce as well as a roux made with all purpose or bread flour. The most commonly used fat is clarified butter, as it has the best flavor. Other fats, such as margarine, oil, lard, and drippings can be used and will impart different flavors, or none at all, to your sauce. You can make any quantity of roux by weighing out equal quantities of flour and fat.

How to Make a Roux

There are three kinds of roux: white, blond, and brown. They are similar in that they all contain equal quantities of flour and fat. They only differ by the length of time that they are cooked. They must all be cooked long enough to enable the fat to cook the flour. If the flour is not cooked long enough, the sauce will taste pasty. A white roux is cooked 2 to 3 minutes and no longer. The mixture should be bubbling and will have a faintly grainy texture. To produce a blond roux, continue cooking a few minutes longer, just until it begins to darken in color. To produce a brown roux, the roux is further cooked over a lower heat until it turns a golden brown. The lower heat will prevent the roux from burning.

Method

- Melt the fat in a saucepan over moderate heat

- Add an equal quantity of flour

- Stir with a wire whisk until well mixed

- Cook over medium heat at least 2 minutes stirring constantly, then longer over low heat until a blond or brown roux develops

- Use immediately, or cool and keep refrigerated

Adding Liquid to the Roux

There are two methods of adding and incorporating liquid into a roux. To thicken two quarts of liquid, you need 6oz (185g) of roux for a thin consistency, 8oz (250g) of roux for a medium consistency, and 12oz (375g) of roux for a thick consistency.

First method

Use this method if you have just made the roux. In this case, the liquid to be added can be hot or cool, but not ice cold. Make sure to cool the roux slightly before adding the liquid. If the roux is too hot, lumps could form.

Method

- Pour the hot or cool liquid gradually into the roux while whisking constantly.

- Bring the liquid to a boil, whisking constantly, then reduce to a simmer.

- Simmer, while whisking occasionally for 20 minutes to 1 hour.

If using the roux right away, place a pat of butter over the surface of the sauce. Once melted it will prevent a skin from forming. Place the pot of sauce in a warm bain-marie to keep warm. Otherwise, cover with cling wrap and keep in the fridge for up to 3 days.

Second method

Use the second method if your roux was stored in the fridge.

Method

- Bring the liquid to a boil then reduce to a simmer.

- Add a small piece of roux and whisk it into the liquid until incorporated and smooth.

- Repeat, adding small pieces of roux and continue whisking until you like the consistency.

- Continue to simmer for a total of 1 hour.

- If your sauce becomes too thick, you can add some liquid until the desired consistency is reached.

Note: Do not use aluminum pots to make sauces, as they will impart a grayish color to the sauce. Heavy bottom, stainless steel pots are best suited to this task.

Béchamel Sauce

Béchamel is the base white sauce used to create secondary (also called small) sauces such as cheddar cheese sauce, mornay sauce, mustard sauce, and cream sauce. A complete list follows with instructions on how to make them.

Recipe for Béchamel Sauce
Makes 4 cups (1 liter)

Ingredients

- 1/4 cup (65g) all-purpose flour

- 1/4 cup (65g) unsalted butter

- 4 cups (1L) milk

- 1/2 small onion, peeled

- 1 whole clove
- 1 bay leaf
- To taste salt, white pepper, nutmeg

Method

- First make a roux by melting the butter over medium heat in a saucepan
- When the butter has melted, add the flour and whisk 2 to 3 minutes over medium heat
- Cool slightly
- Meanwhile, bring the milk just to the scalding point, then add to the roux, stirring vigorously with a whisk until incorporated
- Take the clove and pierce it through the bay leaf and into the onion; drop this into the liquid to add flavor
- Bring the sauce to a boil, whisking constantly, then reduce to a simmer and let it simmer for 20 to 30 minutes, stirring occasionally
- Adjust the thickness to your liking, using hot milk to thin it if necessary
- Taste, and season lightly with salt, white pepper, and nutmeg
- Strain the sauce through a fine mesh strainer or a chinois lined with cheesecloth
- Cover with cling wrap, or place a pat of butter on top to keep a skin from forming
- Cool in a cold water bath and place in the fridge

To produce a secondary (small) sauce, add the following ingredients for each to one quart of béchamel sauce.

Cheddar Cheese Sauce

- 1 cup (250g) cheddar cheese
- 2 tsp (10ml) Worcestershire sauce
- 1/2 tsp (3g) dry mustard

Cream Sauce

- 2/3 – 1 1/8 cup (150 to 250ml) of heated cream (any kind)

Mornay Sauce

- 5oz (125g) grated Gruyere cheese, then remove from heat and add 1/4 cup (60g) butter and a pinch of ground nutmeg

Mustard Sauce

- 5oz (125g) of prepared mustard (Dijon or other)

Soubise Sauce

- Add 2 cups (500g) finely diced onions, sweated in butter over low heat, to the sauce and simmer 20 minutes. Strain the sauce through a fine mesh strainer. Add 1/4 cup (60g) butter (optional).

Tomato Soubise Sauce

- Add 500ml (2 cups) tomato purée to the soubise sauce after straining

Velouté

Velouté is a two-step base sauce that has a few different versions depending on which stock you use:

Step One

Velouté can be made with chicken, veal, or fish stock.

Step Two

Step one velouté produces one of these bases:

White wine sauce

- Traditionally made with fish velouté (chicken velouté is used as well) and heavy cream.

Supreme sauce

- Made with chicken velouté and heavy cream.

Allemande sauce

- Traditionally made with veal velouté (chicken velouté is used as well) and heavy cream.

These sauces are used as a base for many other secondary (small) sauces that we will look at after we have made the various velouté base sauces.

Step One:

Recipe for Velouté
Makes 4 cups (1 liter)

Ingredients

- 4 tbsp (60g) all purpose flour
- 4 tbsp (60g) clarified butter (see end of chapter for procedure to clarify butter)
- 4 cups (1L) white stock (chicken, fish, or veal)

Method

- Melt the butter over medium heat
- Add the flour while whisking constantly over medium heat
- Cook the roux to a blond stage, about 3 to 5 minutes, then cool slightly
- Meanwhile, heat the stock to hot, but not boiling
- Pour the stock gradually into the roux while whisking constantly
- Bring sauce to a boil, whisking constantly, then reduce to a simmer
- Let the sauce simmer over low heat for at least an hour
- Adjust the sauce's consistency at any time by adding some hot stock to thin it out
- Strain the sauce through a fine mesh strainer, or chinois lined with a cheesecloth
- Cover the surface with cling wrap or a pat of butter to keep a skin from forming
- Place in a warm bain-marie if you are going to step two of the velouté sauce, or chill over a cold bain-marie and refrigerate

Step Two Options:

Option One

Recipe for White Wine Sauce
Makes 4 cups (1 liter)

Ingredients

- 2/3 cup (160ml) dry white wine
- 4 cups (1L) fish velouté
- 1/2 cup (125ml) heated heavy cream
- 2 tbsp (30g) cold butter, cut in pieces
- to taste salt, white pepper, lemon juice

Method

- Bring the wine to a boil in a saucepan and reduce the quantity by half
- Add the fish velouté and whisk it into the reduced wine
- Bring to a boil, then reduce to a simmer
- Add the hot cream and whisk to incorporate
- Remove the sauce from the heat and add the cold pieces of butter, one at a time whisking constantly
- Add seasonings to taste
- Strain through a fine mesh strainer or cheesecloth in a chinois
- Cool over a cold bain-marie and keep in the fridge, making sure the surface of the sauce is covered with cling wrap

Option Two

Recipe for Supreme Sauce
Makes 4 cups (1 liter)

Ingredients

- 4 cups (1 liter) chicken velouté
- 2/3 cup (160ml) heavy cream
- 2 tbsp (30g) cold butter, cut in pieces
- to taste salt, white pepper, lemon juice

Method

- Bring the chicken velouté to a simmer, and let simmer until reduced by about a quarter in volume
- Place the cream in a bowl and add a little of the hot velouté to the cream and mix it well (this is called **tempering** the cream)
- Pour the cream mixture into the simmering chicken velouté, and bring it back to a boil, then reduce to a simmer
- Whisk in the cold butter pieces one at a time
- Taste and add the necessary amount of seasonings
- Strain through a fine mesh strainer or through a chinois lined with cheesecloth
- Cover surface with cling wrap and keep warm in a warm bain-marie or cool over a cold bain-marie and refrigerate

Option Three

Recipe for Allemande Sauce:
Makes 4 cups (1 liter)

Ingredients

- 4 cups (1L) veal or chicken velouté
- 1 cup (250ml) heavy cream
- 2 egg yolks
- To taste salt, white pepper, lemon juice

Method

- Bring the velouté to a simmer and reduce by a quarter
- Whisk the egg yolks and the cream together in a bowl, then slowly add a third of the hot sauce into the cream mixture while whisking
- Next, slowly add the cream mixture back into the velouté in the sauce pan, while whisking, until the mixture is incorporated
- Reheat the mixture to simmering. DO NOT BOIL or your sauce will split.
- Taste and add any necessary seasonings
- Cool and cover surface with cling wrap, or keep warm over a warm bain-marie

The following secondary or small sauces are made from 4 cups (1 liter) of velouté, white wine sauce, supreme sauce, or allemande sauce:

Anchovy Sauce

Base sauce: fish velouté
Add 4oz (125ml) mushroom trimmings and 4oz (125ml) oyster liquid. Reduce sauce by a third. Finish with a liaison of 4 egg yolks and 1 cup (250ml) heavy cream. Strain and swirl in 3oz (75g) anchovy butter. (See end of chapter for recipe.)

Aurora Sauce

Base sauce: veal or chicken velouté, or supreme or allemande sauce.
Add 6oz (175g) tomato puree.

Bercy Sauce

Base sauce: fish velouté
Add a 2/3 reduction of 2oz (60g) finely chopped shallots and 1/2 cup (125ml) white wine to the fish velouté. Simmer a few minutes, then whisk in 2oz (60g) cold butter and 2 tbsp (30g) chopped fresh parsley. Add lemon juice, salt, and white pepper to taste.

Curry Sauce

Base sauce: chicken, veal, or fish velouté
Melt 1oz (25g) butter in a pan. Slowly cook 4oz (125g) of mirepoix, cut in a brunoise cut until soft, but not browned. Add 1 crushed garlic clove, 1 tbsp (15g) curry paste or powder, 1/2 bay leaf, 4 parsley stems, and a pinch of thyme, and cook for a couple of minutes. Add the velouté of choice and simmer for 25 minutes. Add 1/2 cup (125ml) heavy cream. Strain. Taste and season with lemon juice, salt, and chervil.

Herb Sauce

Base sauce: white wine sauce
Add chopped fresh herbs to taste. Examples include parsley, chives, tarragon, chervil, and dill. Light herbs are best.

Horseradish Sauce

Base sauce: veal velouté
Add 2oz (60g) drained horseradish, 1/2 cup (125ml) heavy cream, and 2 tsp (10g) dry mustard dissolved in 2 tbsp (30ml) vinegar.

Hungarian Sauce

Base sauce: veal or chicken velouté
Melt 2oz (50g) butter over low heat in a saucepan. Add 2oz (60g) finely diced onion and 1 tbsp (15g) paprika. Sweat the onions 5 minutes over low heat until soft, but not browned. Add 1/2 cup (125ml) white wine and simmer to reduce the mixture by half. Add the velouté and simmer 15 minutes. Strain. Taste and season.

Ivory Sauce

Base sauce: supreme sauce
Add 2oz (60g) glace de viande.

Mushroom Sauce

Base sauce: supreme, allemande, or white wine sauce
Melt 1oz (25g) butter over low heat in a saucepan, add 4oz (125g) sliced white mushrooms and 1 tbsp (15ml) lemon juice (to keep the mushrooms pale). Sauté until cooked. Add to the base sauce. Taste and season with fresh tarragon, salt, and white pepper.

Normandy Sauce

Base sauce: fish velouté
Follow the instructions for anchovy sauce, but add regular cold butter instead of anchovy butter.

Poulette Sauce

Base sauce: allemande sauce
When making allemande sauce, add 8oz (250g) white mushroom trimmings to the cooking sauce. Strain. Add chopped parsley, lemon juice, and seasonings to taste.

Shrimp Sauce

Base sauce: white wine sauce
Add 5oz (125g) shrimp butter (see end of chapter for compound butters) and 1/2 tsp (3g) cayenne pepper. Taste and season.

Venetian Sauce

Base sauce: white wine sauce
Add a 2/3 reduction of 1/2 cup (125ml) tarragon vinegar, 1/2 cup (125ml) white wine, 2oz (60g) finely chopped shallots, and 2 tsp (10g) fresh chervil to the wine sauce. Simmer 3 minutes. Strain. Taste and season with fresh tarragon, salt, and white pepper.

Brown (Espagnole) Sauce

Brown, or Espagnole, sauce is used on its own or added to brown stock to make demi-glace, which is used to make a variety of secondary small sauces. Brown sauce is also used to make Fond

Lie by adding cornstarch as a thickening agent.

Step One:

Making a Brown Sauce (Espagnole Sauce)
Makes 4 cups (1 liter)

Ingredients

- 1/2 cup (125g) medium diced onions
- 4 tbsp (60g) medium diced carrots
- 4 tbsp (60g) medium diced celery
- 4 tbsp (60g) cold butter
- 4 tbsp (60g) all purpose flour
- 6 cups (1.5L) brown stock
- 4 tbsp (60g) tomato purée
- 1 bouquet garni

Method

- Sauté the first three ingredients (mirepoix) in butter until browned
- Add the flour to the mirepoix in the saucepan and stir, continuing to cook until the flour has browned
- Slowly stir in the tomato purée and the brown stock until it is incorporated
- Bring the mixture to a boil, then reduce to a simmer. Add the bouquet garni and simmer 2 to 2 1/2 hours. Skim the surface occasionally
- Strain through a chinois lined with cheesecloth or a fine mesh strainer
- Cover with cling wrap or place a pat of butter to melt over the surface to prevent a skin from forming
- Keep warm in a warm bain-marie, or chill over a cold bain-marie and store in the fridge

Step Two:
Option One:

Fond Lie Sauce
Makes 4 cups (1 liter)

Ingredients

4 cups (1 liter) brown stock

2 tbsp (30g) cornstarch

Method

- Bring the stock to a boil, then reduce to a simmer
- Add a little cold water to the cornstarch to dissolve it
- Whisk the cornstarch mixture into the stock
- Simmer until thickened and clear, and reduce until the desired consistency is reached
- Taste and season

Option Two:

Demi-glace
Makes 4 cups (1 liter)

Ingredients

4 cups (1 liter) brown sauce

4 cups (1 liter) brown stock

Method

- Mix the stock and the sauce in a large stockpot
- Simmer until reduced by about one-half
- Strain through a fine mesh strainer or a chinois lined with cheesecloth
- Taste and season
- Cover and keep warm in a warm bain-marie, or chill over a cold bain-marie, cover with cling wrap, and keep refrigerated.

Step Three:

Secondary Sauces Made with Demi-glace

All of the sauces below are made with a base of 4 cups (1 liter) of demi-glace.

Bercy Sauce _____

Add a 3⁄4 reduction of 1 cup (250ml) dry white wine and 1/2 cup (125g) finely chopped shallots to the demi-glace and simmer 15 minutes.

Bordelaise Sauce _____

Add a 3⁄4 reduction of 1 cup (250 ml) dry red wine, 2oz (60g) finely chopped shallots, 1/4 tsp (1ml) crushed peppercorns, 1⁄2 bay leaf, and a pinch of thyme, to the demi-glace and simmer for 20 minutes. Strain. Stir in 4 tbsp (60g) cold butter. Taste and season.

Charcutiere Sauce _____

Garnish Robert Sauce (see below) with julienne of dill pickles.

Chasseur Sauce _____

Melt 4 tbsp (60g) butter in a sauté pan, add 1/2 cup (125g) sliced mushrooms and 4 tbsp (60g) finely chopped shallots. Sauté until brown. Add 1 cup (250ml) dry white wine and reduce the sauce by 3⁄4. Add the demi-glace and 8oz (250g) finely diced peeled tomato. Simmer 5 minutes and add 2 tsp (10g) chopped parsley. Taste and season.

Diable Sauce _____

Add a 2/3 reduction of 8oz (250ml) dry white wine, 1/2 cup (125g) finely chopped shallots, and 1/2 tsp (2g) crushed peppercorns to the demi-glace sauce, and simmer for 20 minutes. Season with cayenne to taste.

Italian Sauce _____

Melt 2oz (60g) butter in a sauté pan. Add 2 cups (500g) finely chopped mushrooms and 1 tbsp (15g) finely chopped shallots, and sauté until all moisture is evaporated from the mixture. Add 1 cup (250ml) dry white wine and reduce by half. Add 2 tbsp (30g) tomato paste and the demi-glace, and simmer 15 minutes. Add 2 tbsp (30g) chopped fresh parsley. Taste and season.

Lyonnaise Sauce _____

Melt 4 tbsp (60g) butter in a sauté pan. Add 1/2 cup (125g) diced onions and cook until lightly browned. Add 1/2 cup (125ml) white wine vinegar and reduce by half. Add the demi-glace and simmer 15 minutes. Taste and season.

Madeira Sauce _____

Simmer the demi-glace and reduce by 1/2 cup (100ml). Add 4oz (100ml) Madeira wine. Taste and season.

Marchand de Vin _____

Add a 3⁄4 reduction of 6oz (200ml) red wine and 4 tbsp (60g) finely chopped shallots to the demi-glace sauce. Simmer 10 minutes. Strain. Taste and season.

Mushroom Sauce

Melt 4 tbsp (60g) butter in a sauté pan. Add 1 cup (250g) sliced mushrooms and 2 tbsp (30g) finely chopped shallots and sauté until browned. Add the demi-glace and simmer 15 minutes. Add 2oz (60ml) sherry and a few drops of lemon juice. Taste and season.

Perigueux Sauce

Add 1 tbsp (15g) chopped truffles to Madeira sauce.

Piquante Sauce

Add a 2/3 reduction of 1/2 cup (125g) finely diced shallots, 4oz (125ml) wine vinegar, and 4oz (125ml) white wine, to the demi-glace. Simmer 5 minutes. Add 4 tbsp (60g) capers, 4 tbsp (60g) dill pickles (small dice), 1 tbsp (15g) chopped parsley, and 1/2 tsp (2g) tarragon. Taste and season.

Poivrade Sauce

Melt 1/2 cup (125g) butter in a saucepan. Brown 2 cups (500g) mirepoix in the pan. Add 4oz (125ml) red wine, and 3 cups (750ml) basic marinade for meat and simmer until reduced by half. Add the demi-glace and reduce by 1/3, simmering over low heat. Add 1/2 tsp (2g) crushed peppercorns and simmer 10 minutes. Strain. Taste and season.

Port Wine Sauce

Simmer the demi-glace and reduce by 1/2 cup (125ml). Add 4oz (100ml) port wine. Taste and season.

Robert Sauce

Melt 4 tbsp (60g) butter in a saucepan. Add 1/2 cup (125g) finely chopped onion and cook over low heat 5 minutes without browning. Add 1 cup (250ml) white wine. Reduce the sauce by 2/3, simmering over low heat. Add the demi-glace and continue simmering for 10 minutes. Strain. Taste and season.

Tomato Sauce

Recipe for Tomato Sauce
Makes 2 cups (500ml)

Ingredients:

- 4 tbsp (60g) finely chopped garlic
- 6 tbsp (90g) finely chopped onion or shallots
- 4 tbsp (60ml) olive oil
- 3 cups (750g) peeled, seeded, and chopped tomatoes
- salt, pepper to taste

Method

- Cook the garlic and onions or shallots in the olive oil over low heat until soft, but not brown
- Add the tomatoes and cook until the liquid in the tomatoes has evaporated and the sauce is a consistency to your liking
- Taste and season

Secondary Sauces Made from Tomato Sauce

To produce each of the following sauces add the ingredients listed to 2 cups (500ml) of tomato sauce.

Creole Sauce

In 4 tbsp (60g) olive oil, sauté 4 tbsp (60g) finely diced onions, 4 tbsp (60g) finely chopped celery, 2 tbsp (30g) finely diced green pepper, and 1 tsp (5g) finely chopped garlic. Add the tomato sauce, 1 tsp (5g) thyme, one bay leaf, and 1/2 tsp (3g) grated lemon rind. Simmer 25 minutes over low heat. Remove from heat, and discard the bay leaf. Taste. Season with cayenne.

Portuguese Sauce

In 2 tbsp (30ml) olive oil, sauté 4 tbsp (60g) small diced onions, add 1 cup (250g) diced tomatoes and 1 tsp (5g) crushed garlic. Simmer until reduced by 1/3. Add the tomato sauce and 2 tbsp (30g) chopped parsley. Taste and season.

Spanish Sauce

In 4 tbsp (60g) olive oil, sauté over low heat for 6 minutes: 4 tbsp (60g) small diced onion, 4 tbsp (60g) small diced green pepper, 4 tbsp (60g) sliced mushrooms, and 1 small clove of garlic, finely chopped. Add the tomato sauce and a dash of hot red pepper sauce. Taste and season.

Hollandaise Sauce

Hollandaise sauce is a butter sauce thickened with eggs. It is a delicate sauce and requires careful preparation, or it will not hold together properly. With a little practice you will find it is not hard to make, but a very specific method is required. This sauce uses a cooking technique called **emulsion**, which is combining two liquids that do not normally combine well into a smooth liquid. This is accomplished by whisking, which produces many little air bubbles and allows the two mixtures to blend. It is important not to overheat the sauce. This will cause the eggs to split and your sauce to become lumpy.

Hollandaise sauce must be made as required because it does not keep well in the fridge or freezer. Prepare only what you will use immediately. If left at room temperature for any length of time, it becomes a perfect conduit for bacteria growth.

Recipe for Hollandaise Sauce

Ingredients

- 1 lb (450g) warm (not hot) clarified butter
- 6 egg yolks
- 2 tbsp (30g) cold water
- 3 tbsp (50ml) lemon juice
- to taste: salt, white pepper, cayenne pepper

Method

- In a stainless steel, round-bottom bowl, place the egg yolks and the cold water. Whisk well

- Add a few drops of lemon juice and whisk together

- Place the bowl over a hot water bain-marie, and continue to whisk until the mixture is thick and leaves a trail when you lift out the whisk

- Remove the bowl from the bain-marie and very slowly, drop by drop, and then gradually faster, add the warm butter to the egg mixture while constantly whisking until the butter is incorporated

- Taste and season with lemon juice, salt, and white pepper. If the sauce is too thick for your liking, dilute it slightly by adding some warm water a little at a time

- Keep warm in a warm bain-marie, and do not keep for longer than 90 minutes for food safety reasons. Discard after 90 minutes

- Be careful not to overheat, as the sauce may split

How to rescue a split sauce:

When a sauce splits, first try adding a teaspoon of cold water and whisking to see if it comes back together. If that doesn't work, use new egg yolks, and repeat the recipe, adding the sauce where you would have added the butter.

Béarnaise Sauce _____

Béarnaise sauce is a variation of Hollandaise sauce.

The method is the same, however, along with the egg yolks, add a cooled, 3⁄4 reduction of 2 tbsp (30g) finely chopped shallots, 1/2 cup (125ml) white wine vinegar, 1 tsp (5g) fresh chopped tarragon and 1/2 tsp (3g) crushed black peppercorns. Follow the instructions for Hollandaise sauce. Strain the sauce, then taste and season with lemon juice, salt, pepper, cayenne, chopped parsley, chopped tarragon, and chopped chervil.

Secondary Sauces Made from Hollandaise or Béarnaise Sauce:

Choron Sauce _____

Add 4 tbsp (60g) tomato paste and whisk into 2 cups (500ml) Béarnaise sauce.

Foyot Sauce _____

Add 4 tbsp (60g) melted meat glaze (glace de viande) to 2 cups (500ml) Béarnaise sauce.

Maltaise Sauce _____

Add 2oz (60ml) orange juice and 1 tsp (5g) grated orange rind to 2 cups (500ml) Hollandaise sauce.

Mousseline Sauce _____

Whip 1/2 cup (125ml) whipping cream until stiff peaks form, then fold the whipped cream gently into 2 cups (500ml) of Hollandaise sauce. Add cayenne pepper and lemon juice to taste.

Other Sauces

There are many other sauces and new sauces are always being created. These fall into broad categories such as butter sauces, flavored oils, puréses (coulis), and gravies.

Flavored Oils

Flavored oils are oils infused with the flavor of herbs, spices, flowers, fruits, and vegetables. They have become popular as a lighter substitute for heavy sauces. They are usually drizzled lightly over the food or on the plate in a decorative pattern. They can also be used as salad dressings.

Method

- Use light oils like canola, corn, grape seed, safflower, or light olive oil

- Prepare flavoring ingredients in the following manner:

Dried or Ground Spices
Heat slowly in a bit of the oil over low heat until you can smell the aroma of the spices (mustard, cumin, cinnamon, ginger)

Fresh Mild Herbs
Blanch in boiling water for 10 seconds, then drain and refresh under cold water. Dry well using paper towel (parsley, chives, tarragon, chervil, basil, cilantro)

Citrus Zest
Grate with a fine grater or rasp

Fresh Roots or Strong Herbs
Chop finely in a food mill or by hand. (garlic, ginger, horseradish, shallots, rosemary, sage, thyme, oregano)

- Add oil to the flavoring ingredients in a sealable container

- Seal the container and shake it well. Keep at room temperature for 30 minutes shaking occasionally, then store in fridge

- Depending on the flavor you have added, the oil will gradually take on the flavor. Taste the oil until you are happy with the flavor, then filter the oil through a coffee filter and store in an airtight container in the fridge

❖ Lemon	❖ Parsley
❖ Orange	❖ Chervil
❖ Garlic	❖ Cilantro
❖ Shallot	❖ Basil
❖ Ginger	❖ Oregano
❖ Horseradish	❖ Cinnamon
❖ Rosemary	❖ Cumin
❖ Sage	❖ Curry
❖ Thyme	❖ Paprika

Gravies

Gravy is a sauce made from the drippings of roasted meat or poultry. Basically, gravies are pan juices thickened with roux and flavored with stock or water, milk or cream, and seasonings.

Jus is unthickened pan juices from the roasting pan, sometimes with stock added to increase the original amount.

Method

- Remove the roast from the roasting pan
- Spoon the fat from the top of the drippings until only a small amount remains
- Add flour to the pan and whisk to make a roux
- Cook 3 to 5 minutes
- Add stock to the pan and whisk to incorporate
- Bring to a boil, then simmer and reduce until desired thickness is reached
- Strain through a fine mesh strainer
- Taste and season

There is no specific quantity to list as every roast will have a different quantity of drippings in the pan. You will learn by practice. Remember a roux has equal portions of fat and flour; therefore, use your judgment to estimate the approximate quantity of fat in the pan and add the equivalent amount of flour. Usually 1/2 cup (125g) of flour and 2 cups (500ml) of liquid, stock, or water will be enough.

Butter Sauces

Butter is a wonderful ingredient with which to create simple or complex sauces. In a professional kitchen there is always butter in the fridge, and a simple delicious butter sauce can be made in a few minutes.

Melted Butter

This simplest of sauces is great to pour over vegetables. Just season to taste, with perhaps a little lemon or orange juice and some fresh chopped light herbs to create a rich, delicious sauce.

Brown Butter

If you continue to cook melted butter, it will turn brown and acquire a nutty flavor. This is called *beurre noisette*, French for "nut butter." This is usually made at the time of service and poured over fish or vegetables.

Clarified Butter

Clarified butter is made from regular butter through a process that removes the water and milk solids. The result is a clear butter, which is ideal for sautéing foods. Because the milk solids have been removed, the butter will not scorch when heated to high temperatures. To clarify butter, melt the butter over low heat. Skim the froth from the surface of the butter and gently pour the clear butter away from the solids.

Compound Butters

Compound butters are a variety of flavored butters made by adding both fresh and cooked ingredients to softened butter. The ingredients and butter are mixed together, then chilled, often formed into a variety of decorative shapes. Pieces of the butter are used at the time of serving, designed to melt just as the dish is brought to the diner. They may also be stirred into sauces at the last minute for extra flavor.

Procedure for Making Compound Butters

Add the following ingredients to 1 lb (450g) of butter:

Anchovy Butter

Add 4 tbsp (60g) anchovy paste

Curry Butter

Add either 1 tbsp (15ml) curry paste or 4 tsp (20g) curry powder, heat gently in the butter, then cool

Escargot (Snail Butter)

Add 2 tbsp (30g) garlic paste, 1/2 cup (125g) chopped parsley, salt and white pepper to taste

Garlic Butter

Add 2 tbsp (30g) garlic paste

Herb Butter

Add 1/2 cup (125g) fresh chopped herbs to taste

Hotel Butter (Maitre d'Hotel Butter)

Add 1/4 cup (60g) chopped parsley, 1 1/2oz (50ml) lemon juice, white pepper

Mustard Butter

Add 4 tbsp (60g) Dijon mustard, grainy or smooth

Scallion Butter

Add 4 tbsp (60g) chopped scallions

Shallot Butter

Add 4 tbsp (60g) finely chopped shallots

Shrimp Butter

Place 1 cup (250g) cooked shrimp (with shell) and butter into a food processor and pulse to a fine grind. Push through a fine mesh strainer to remove the shell pieces.

Beurre Blanc

Beurre blanc is a butter sauce made by whisking cold butter into a hot vinegar reduction to make an emulsion sauce. This sauce is usually made just before serving.

Recipe for Beurre Blanc Sauce
Makes 2 cups (500ml)

Ingredients:
- 8 oz (250ml) dry white wine
- 1 1/2 oz (50ml) white wine vinegar
- 2 tbsp (30g) finely chopped shallots
- 1 lb (450g) cold butter cut in small pieces
- to taste: salt, white pepper

Method
- In a saucepan, add the wine, vinegar, and shallots and bring to a simmer
- Reduce until only 1 oz (30ml) of liquid remains
- Add small pieces of cold butter into the sauce while whisking continuously. When only a few pieces of butter remain, remove the pan from the heat
- Whisk in the last few pieces of butter and continue to whisk until completely smooth. Strain. Taste and season

Variations on Beurre Blanc:

Beurre Rouge

Use dry red wine and red wine vinegar instead of white wine and white wine vinegar.

Herbed Beurre Blanc

Add fresh chopped herbs to the beurre blanc.

More Sauces

Vinaigrettes, Aiolis, Pestos, Chutneys, Dips, and Dressings

These are all sometimes used as sauces on today's menus as lighter and healthier dishes are popular.

The following are some examples of other sauces:

> ### Tartar Sauce
> (dressing for fish)
>
> ### Horseradish Sauce
> (dressing for cold meats)
>
> ### Cocktail Sauce
> (dressing for shrimp)
>
> ### Mignonette Sauce
> (dressing for oysters)
>
> ### Barbecue Sauce
> (basting sauce for barbecued meats)

Chapter 12
Questions...

1. A sauce can enhance the taste and visual perception of a dish. Provide an example of each.

2. Which of these sauces are base sauces?

   a. Espagnole sauce
   b. mornay sauce
   c. béchamel sauce
   d. tomato sauce

3. What is the ratio of butter to flour in a roux?

4. Name two secondary sauces made from béchamel sauce.

5. Velouté can be made with which of the following stocks?

   a. fish
   b. veal
   c. chicken
   d. lamb

6. Which of the following two ingredients make a Fond Lie sauce?

   a. chicken stock and flour
   b. brown stock and cornstarch
   c. veal stock and roux
   d. fish stock and cornstarch

7. Hollandaise is a butter sauce thickened with _____.

   a. Roux
   b. Cornstarch
   c. Eggs
   d. None of the above

8. Name two kinds of compound butter.

CHAPTER 13

Soups

Soups originated in peasant cooking and have been an important part of most traditional cuisines around the world. Although soups have traditionally been rather basic, many have been elevated to the level of haute cuisine, and some can be found on even the priciest of menus. Soup is considered by many to be healthy and comforting, so it is a popular menu item, especially in cold winter months.

The potential for creative flavors in soup making is endless, and the possibility for profit making is attractive. Many chefs have used canned soups and prepackaged products, believing this will save them time and money. In fact, it can be quite the opposite. Soups made from scratch can feed a crowd quite inexpensively and are vastly superior products. They are versatile and economical, as they can be varied to include whatever ingredients you have on hand. From this, you can reason that investing time in making excellent soups will enhance your culinary reputation and increase your profits!

As in making stocks, the final product is only as good as the ingredients you put into it. Do not use food that belongs in the waste bin.

Most soup can be made ahead of time and reheated at the time of service. It is also advisable to make soup in large quantities, so you can store some in the freezer for future use.

Soups can be made from just about any ingredient available. They can also be either hot or cold. It is therefore difficult to classify soups in a rigid way. However, most soups will fall into one of the following categories: clear light soups, opaque thickened soups, or specialty soups (the default category).

Soups can be served as a starter, a main course, or even as a dessert. The portion size is usually 6–8 ounces (200–250 ml) for a starter and 10–12 ounces (300–350 ml) for a main course. Dessert soups are usually served in very small portions—about 4–5 ounces (125 ml).

When making great soups, one must place a definite focus on presentation. Soups benefit greatly from some attractive garnishes. Garnishing is the art of adding decorative items (some edible, but not always) to enhance the presentation and flavor of a dish. Garnishes must complement the soup but not overpower it.

Kinds of Soup

Thick Opaque Soup

There are two categories of thick opaque soup. Cream soups are thickened with a thickening agent, such as a roux, and have cream added to them. They are rich-tasting soups and are usually named after the main ingredient, such as cream of broccoli or cream of chicken. Heavier versions, like chowders and bisques, have pieces of meat, seafood, and/or vegetables added to them. Puréed soups are thickened naturally by the blending of ingredients in a food processor. Often, starchy vegetables like potatoes or cooked rice are included to aid in the thickening process. Once puréed, cream or milk is often added.

Clear Soups

The base of clear soups is stock. Many different ingredients can then be added. Chicken noodle soup and beef and barley soup are two well-known examples of clear soup. Consommés are clear soups made by a process of clarifying stocks and condensing flavors. They require careful effort, and are therefore not offered frequently on current menus.

Clear Vegetable Soups

Clear vegetable soups may seem simple; however, the quality of ingredients and the right preparation are very important. One must start with a good-quality vegetable, poultry, or brown stock. Many combinations of vegetables, grains, rice, herbs, and seasonings can then be added.

When preparing the vegetables, cut them into uniform sizes so they will finish cooking at the same time. Bite-size pieces are ideal, as diners do not enjoy huge pieces of food that are difficult to manage. Starchy vegetables may cause a soup to turn cloudy, so it may be necessary to cook them separately and add them just before serving. Cook denser vegetables longer, adding delicate vegetables toward the end of cooking. Be careful not to overcook the vegetables, or they can become mushy.

Always add seasonings at the end of the cooking process, after tasting. Delicate herbs should also be added just before serving. Once cooked, do not allow the soup to boil away endlessly on the stove. Chill the soup over a cold bain-marie or in the sink, and reheat smaller quantities as needed. Use your culinary judgment to decide what garnishes can be added to enhance the flavor and presentation.

French Onion Soup
Serves 4

- 2 tbsp (30g) butter
- 4 cups (1kg) thinly sliced onions
- 2 sprigs fresh thyme
- 1 bay leaf
- 4 cups (1L) beef stock
- 12 oz (340ml) beer
- to taste: salt and freshly ground black pepper
- 12 thin slices of french bread (baguette), toasted
- 1 1/2 cups (375g) gruyère cheese, shredded

Procedure for Cooking:
- Melt butter over medium heat in a stockpot
- Add the onions and cook, stirring frequently until brown, 10 to 12 minutes
- Add the thyme, bay leaf, beer, and stock
- Bring to a boil, cover, and reduce to a simmer for 20 to 25 minutes
- Remove bay leaf and thyme
- Ladle the soup into ovenproof bowls or ramekins
- Place the toasted baguette slices over the surface of the soup and sprinkle generously with the shredded cheese
- Place under the broiler to brown the cheese until it is bubbling and melted
- Serve immediately

Barley Soup
Serves 6

- 1 cup (250g) pearl barley
- 2 tbsp (30ml) olive oil
- 5 small (or 3 large) onions, minced
- 2 cloves garlic, minced
- 2 tbsp (30g) fresh parsley, chopped
- 1/4 cup (65g) bacon, finely chopped
- 2 cups (500ml) stock (chicken, brown, or vegetable)
- to taste: salt and freshly ground black pepper

Procedure for Cooking:
- Cover the barley in water and soak overnight
- Discard any grains that have floated to the surface of the water
- Drain and rinse the barley under cold running water
- Heat the oil in a stockpot over medium heat
- Add the onions, garlic, and bacon, and sauté about 5 minutes, stirring occasionally until the mixture begins to color
- Add the barley and stir
- Cover with stock
- Bring to a boil, cover, and reduce to a simmer for about 1 1/2 hours until barley is tender
- Taste and season with salt and pepper
- Add the parsley just prior to serving

Red Lentil Soup
Serves 4

- 1 1/2 cups (340g) red lentils
- 7 cups (1.75L) water
- 1 large (or 2 small) onion, chopped
- 2 cloves garlic, minced
- 1 tsp (5g) ground coriander
- 1 tsp (5g) ground cumin
- 1/4 tsp (1g) turmeric
- 2 large carrots, halved lengthwise and sliced thinly
- 1 medium red bell pepper, chopped
- 1/4 cup (60g) fresh coriander, washed, dried, and chopped
- 1/4 cup (60g) green onion, chopped
- to taste: salt, pepper, cayenne, fresh
- coriander (cilantro) sprigs, to garnish

Procedure for Cooking:

- In a stockpot, bring the lentils and water to a boil
- Skim the froth that rises to the surface, and discard it
- Stir in the onions, garlic, ground coriander, cumin, and turmeric
- Reduce to a simmer for 20 minutes
- Stir in carrots and simmer 5 minutes more
- Stir in red peppers and simmer until vegetables are cooked
- Stir in fresh coriander, green onions, and cayenne
- Taste and season with salt and pepper
- Serve hot with a garnish of fresh coriander sprigs

French Onion Soup

Barley Soup

Red Lentil Soup

Clear Meat, Poultry, and Seafood Soups

These soups are similar to clear vegetable soups but contain added ingredients such as meat, seafood, or poultry. Chicken noodle soup, a very popular soup in North America, falls into this category. The secret to successful soups containing meat is to cook each ingredient to the proper doneness without overcooking. Uniform, bite-size pieces will aid in even cooking. Add ingredients at the appropriate time, so as not to overcook vegetables or undercook meat.

Shrimp and Vegetable Soup
Serves 4

- 8 large tiger shrimp, peeled and deveined
- 1 small onion, diced
- 2 cloves garlic, minced
- 1 cup (250ml) celery, finely chopped
- 3 leeks, chopped and washed, white parts only
- 2 tbsp (30ml) olive oil
- 1 cup (250ml) dry white wine
- 3 cups (750ml) fish stock
- 4 sprigs fresh parsley
- 1 sprig fresh thyme
- 1 bay leaf, crushed
- 2 tbsp fresh parsley, chopped, to garnish

Procedure for Cooking:

- Rinse the tiger shrimp under cold running water; drain
- Heat the oil in a saucepan over medium heat, then sauté the onion, garlic, leeks, and celery for 4 minutes until soft and clear
- Stir in the wine and simmer 3 minutes to reduce
- Add the stock, parsley sprigs, thyme, and bay leaf, and bring to a boil
- Add the tiger shrimp
- Reduce to a simmer for 3 minutes
- Taste, and season with salt and pepper
- Ladle soup with two tiger shrimp per bowl, top up with more soup, and garnish with fresh chopped parsley

Consommé

Consommé is a clear liquid that is made by clarifying and condensing stocks. A mixture of ground meat, egg whites, and vegetables is added to the cold stock, which is then brought to a boil. The added ingredients help to collect the proteins and coagulants within the stock to render a very clear and pure liquid. Once the mixture is brought to a boil, it is reduced to a simmer. While simmering, the impurities in the mixture float to the surface of the pot, creating a crust on top of the stock. This crust is called a raft. The clarified liquid is gently removed from beneath the raft. The clarified liquid is now called consommé. A pot specially designed for this purpose has a spigot at the bottom to release the consommé from under the raft. Once collected, the consommé is strained through a fine mesh strainer and degreased. Consommé is usually served on its own or with a simple garnish. Historically, it was common for gelatin to be added and for the consommé to be served cold and jellied; however, this is rarely seen on today's menus.

Consommé
Makes 8 2/3 cups (2 liters)

- 8 2/3 cups (2L) brown stock, cold
- 1/4 lb (115g) lean ground beef
- 2 oz (60g) white onion, chopped
- 1 oz (30g) celery, chopped
- 1 1/4 cups (300g) carrots, chopped
- 2 egg whites
- 2 tomatoes, chopped
- 1 leek, chopped, white parts only
- 1 parsley stem, 1 bay leaf
- pinch crushed peppercorns

Procedure for Cooking:
- Add the cold brown stock to a large stockpot (with a spigot, if possible)
- Add ground beef, mirepoix (chopped) vegetables, tomatoes, leeks, herbs, egg whites, and seasonings, and stir well together
- Heat over low heat, stirring occasionally, until the mixture comes to a gentle simmer
- As the mixture simmers, do not disturb the raft on top that forms from the impurities
- Simmer gently 1 1/2 hours

- Remove the stock that is under the raft, by either draining through the spigot or gently scooping with a ladle from under the raft
- Let the stock drain through the mesh strainer, without forcing it
- Degrease the surface of the stock with a paper towel or spoon
- When all obvious grease is removed, taste, and season with salt and white pepper

Variations:
- Add 2 oz (60ml) sherry or port per quart (liter) of consommé
- Double the quantity of celery for a different flavor
- Double the quantity of the tomatoes for a different flavor
- Garnish with cooked meatballs
- Use chicken stock and ground chicken for chicken consommé
- Add vermicelli noodles

Puréed Soups

Puréed soups typically have a base of a root vegetable or sometimes meat. Once the ingredients have cooked for 20 to 40 minutes, the soup is puréed in a food processor or blender until smooth. Add fresh herbs just prior to puréeing. Immersion blenders are ideal for puréeing, as one can place them right into the soup pot, which is preferable to pouring hot liquids into the blender.

Curried Butternut Squash and Pear Soup
Serves 4

- 4 tbsp (60ml) butter

- 2 cups (450g) onions, finely chopped

- 2 tsp (10ml) curry paste

- 2 medium butternut squash (about 3 pounds, or 1.35kg)

- 3 pears, peeled, cored, and chopped

- 4 cups (1L) chicken or vegetable stock

- 1 cup (250ml) pear juice

- to taste: salt and freshly ground black pepper

Procedure for Cooking:

- Melt the butter in a stockpot

- Add the chopped onions and the curry paste, and sweat the mixture over low heat for 15 minutes until onions are clear and cooked

- Peel the squash with a vegetable peeler, scrape out the pulp and seeds, and cut the squash into large pieces

- When the onion mixture is cooked, add the stock, the squash pieces, and the pears to the pot

- Bring to a boil, then partially cover and reduce to a simmer

- Simmer 25 minutes, until squash and pears are cooked through

- Cool slightly, and pour through a strainer.

- Place the solids and 1 cup (250ml) of liquid into a food processor, keeping the remaining liquid to the side

- Purée the solids until smooth

- Return the purée to the pot with the pear juice, and add the cooking liquid until you reach the desired consistency

- Taste, and season with salt and pepper

- As a variation, add 1/4 cup (60ml) of heavy cream after puréeing

Carrot, Ginger, and Orange Soup
Serves 4

- 4 tbsp (60ml) butter
- 2 cups (450g) shallots, finely chopped
- 2 tbsp (30g) fresh ginger, peeled and grated
- 2 1/4 lb (1kg; about 12) carrots, peeled and chopped
- 4 cups (1L) chicken or vegetable stock
- 1 cup (250ml) fresh orange juice
- to taste: salt and black pepper
- to taste: orange zest, freshly grated

Procedure for Cooking:

- Melt the butter in a stockpot
- Add the shallots and ginger and sweat over low heat, stirring occasionally for 10 to 20 minutes, until cooked and clear
- Add the carrots, stock, and orange juice to the onion mixture
- Bring to a boil, cover, then reduce to a simmer and cook until the carrots are tender, about 30 minutes
- Pour the soup through a strainer, and transfer the solids to a food processor, keeping the liquid to the side
- Purée the solids with 1 cup (250ml) of the cooking liquid, until smooth
- Pour the contents of the processor into a clean stockpot, adding only as much cooking liquid as needed until you reach the desired consistency
- Taste, and season with salt, pepper, and orange zest

Oven-Roasted Tomato Soup
Serves 4

- 1 lb (450g) ripe red tomatoes
- 1 clove garlic, finely chopped
- 1 small bunch fresh basil leaves
- 1 small potato, peeled and chopped
- 2 cups (500ml) water, boiling
- 1 tbsp (15ml) tomato paste
- 1 tsp (5ml) balsamic vinegar
- 2 tbsp (30ml) olive oil
- to taste: salt and freshly ground black pepper
- 4 leaves fresh basil, to garnish

Procedure for Cooking:

- Immerse the tomatoes in boiling water for 1 minute

- Remove the tomatoes from the water and peel off the skins

- Slice each tomato in half and arrange on a baking dish, cut side up; season with salt and pepper

- Drizzle the vinegar and a little olive oil over each tomato half, and then sprinkle the chopped garlic

- Dip basil leaves in olive oil and place one over each tomato half

- Place the tomatoes in a preheated oven at 375°F (190°C) and roast for 50 to 60 minutes, until the edges are slightly blackened

- About 20 minutes before the tomatoes are done, put the potato in a saucepan with the boiling water, salt, and tomato paste

- Simmer this mixture for 20 minutes

- When the tomatoes are ready, scrape all contents of the baking dish into a food processor

- Add the contents of the saucepan to the food processor as well

- Purée until smooth

- Pass the soup through a fine mesh strainer to remove the tomato seeds

- Garnish with fresh basil leaves and serve

Chilled Tomato, Cucumber, and Cantaloupe Soup
Serves 6

- 6 ripe tomatoes, peeled and seeded

- 2 medium ripe cantaloupes, peeled and seeded

- 2 large cucumbers, peeled and seeded zest of 1 orange

- 1/4 cup (60g) fresh mint, chopped

- 1 cup (250ml) sour cream

- 12 leaves fresh mint, to garnish

Procedure for Cooking:

- In a food processor, combine the tomatoes, cantaloupe, and cucumber

- Purée until smooth

- Place the mixture in a bowl

- Stir in the sour cream, 1/4 cup chopped mint, and orange zest

- Chill 2 hours

- Serve chilled, with a garnish of fresh mint

Cream Soups and Chowders

Making a cream soup requires many of the same techniques we use to make cream sauces. Like the sauces, the soups are thickened with a thickening agent such as a roux. The flavors are added, then the soup is blended, strained, and seasoned. The consistency of the soup is adjusted with hot cream or milk. As in sauce making, it is important to obtain the right texture, taste, and consistency. One wants to avoid soups that are too thick or too thin. Ideally, cream soup should taste of the featured ingredient—not just cream—and should not be overly spicy. Cream soups are similar to chowders in ingredients, but not in consistency: the former are smooth, whereas the latter contain chunks of vegetables, meat, or seafood.

Some Tips for Making Excellent Cream Soups:

- Always heat the milk or cream before adding it to the soup
- Always thicken the soup before adding the milk or cream
- Make sure your thickening agent has been cooked at least one minute before you add your milk or cream
- Always pass your soup through a fine mesh strainer to achieve a smooth texture
- Always taste and adjust seasonings after adding milk or cream
- To keep the soup from splitting, never boil the soup after you have added the milk or cream

- Use an immersion blender, if possible, to avoid transfer of hot liquid
- Keep your soup pot on the back burner, for safety reasons

Cream of Cauliflower and Stilton Soup
Serves 12

- 1 lb (450g) cauliflower florets, blanched
- 4 oz (120g) shallots, finely diced
- 1 oz (30g) butter
- 4 oz (120g) flour
- 8 2/3 cups (2L) white stock or vegetable stock
- 2 cups (500ml) hot milk or cream
- 8 oz (225g) stilton or blue cheese
- to taste: salt and pepper
- 12 whole chives, chopped, to garnish

Procedure for Cooking:
- Melt the butter in a soup pot

- Add the shallots and sweat 6 minutes, until translucent

- Add the blanched cauliflower

- Add the flour and cook for 2 minutes, but do not brown

- Add the stock, and whisk while bringing to a boil

- Simmer 10 minutes until the vegetables are cooked but not mushy

- Skim any grease off the top

- Purée the soup in an immersion blender or a food processor

- Strain the soup through a fine mesh strainer to remove lumps

- Add the cheese and hot milk or cream until the soup has reached desired consistency

- Taste, and add seasonings

- Serve hot (but do not boil)

- Garnish with chopped chives

Haddock Chowder
Serves 6

- 3/4 lb (340g) haddock fillets, cut into 1/2-inch cubes

- 4 1/3 cups (1L) fish stock

- 1/4 lb (100g) bacon, diced

- 3/4 cup (200g) white onion, diced

- 3/4 cup (200g) diced celery

- 3 tbsp (40g) flour

- 1 cup (250g) potatoes, diced

- 3 cups (720ml) hot milk

- 1/2 cup (125ml) heavy cream, heated

- to taste: salt and pepper

Procedure for Cooking:

- Add the diced bacon to a stockpot and sauté over medium heat until the fat is rendered

- Add the diced onion and celery, and cook 5 minutes until tender, but not brown

- Add the flour, stir to form a roux, and cook 4 minutes; avoid browning it

- Whisk in the cold fish stock

- Bring to a boil while stirring constantly, then reduce to a simmer

- Add the potatoes and simmer until they are tender

- Stir in the hot milk and cream and heat through, but do not boil

- Add the fish pieces and let cook, without boiling, 5 minutes until the fish is cooked through

- Taste, season, and serve

Bisques

Bisques are cream soups that are usually made from shellfish. They are usually thicker than other cream soups because they often contain and a heavy, rich-tasting cream. Some menus incorrectly apply the word bisque to other soups to make them sound more upscale or to justify a higher price.

Lobster Tail Bisque
Serves 8

- 2 tbsp (30g) butter
- 1/4 cup (60g) shallots, diced
- 1/4 cup (60g) carrots, finely diced
- 1/4 cup (60g) celery, diced
- 1 lb (450g) lobster tail, cut into bite-size pieces
- 1 bay leaf
- pinch thyme
- 2 tbsp (30g) tomato paste
- 3 tbsp (45ml) cognac
- 1 cup (250ml) dry white wine
- 4 1/3 cups (1L) fish velouté
- 2 cups (500ml) fish stock
- 1 cup (250ml) heavy cream, heated
- to taste: salt and white pepper
- 1/4 cup (60g) fresh parsley, chopped, to garnish

Procedure for Cooking:

- Add the cognac to a saucepan and heat until nearly boiling
- Standing away from it, carefully light it with a match and allow the cognac to flame until the alcohol content is burned off and the flame is extinguished
- Set aside pan
- In another, large saucepan, melt the butter over medium heat
- Add the shallots, celery, and carrots, and sauté until lightly browned
- Add the lobster tail pieces and herbs, and sauté until the shells turn bright red
- Add the tomato paste and stir well
- Add the burnt cognac and the wine and simmer until reduced by half
- Remove the lobster tails and peel off the shells
- Put the shells back in the saucepan, and reserve the lobster meat for later
- Add the fish stock and the fish velouté, and simmer for 15 minutes
- Strain through a fine mesh strainer
- Return to a simmer
- At the time of service, add the hot cream and lobster pieces
- Warm 1 minute and serve immediately
- Garnish with fresh chopped parsley

Answer key p.180

Chapter 13
Questions...

1. True or **False**: It is expensive and time-consuming to make your own soup.

2. True or **False**: Vegetables past their prime are ideal for soup making.

3. Puréed soups may be thickened with _____.
   a. potatoes
   b. rice
   c. sweet potatoes
   d all of the above

4. Bisques are typically made from _____.
   a. snails
   b. poultry
   c. shellfish
   d. meat

5. To prevent a cream soup from splitting, what is the most important thing to avoid?

6. How does a chowder differ from a cream soup?

Equivalency Charts and Tables

Volume Measurements (Dry)

Milliliters	Teaspoons, Tablespoons & Cups
.5ml	1/8 teaspoon
1ml	1/4 teaspoon
2ml	1/2 teaspoon
4ml	3/4 teaspoon
5ml	1 teaspoon
15ml	1 tablespoon
25ml	2 tablespoons
50ml	1/4 cup
75ml	1/3 cup
125ml	1/2 cup
150ml	2/3 cup
175ml	3/4 cup
250ml	1 cup
500ml	2 cups or 1 pint
750ml	3 cups
1L	4 cups or 1 quart

Volume Measurements Cups to Grams (*per item basis*)

Ingredients in Cups	1/8	1/4	1/3	3/8	1/2	5/8	2/3
Almonds, ground	20g	40g	55g	65g	85g	105g	110g
Almonds, slivered	10g	20g	25g	30g	40g	50g	55g
Butter/margarine	30g	55g	75g	85g	115g	140g	150g
Cocao	15g	30g	40g	45g	60g	70g	75g
Coconut flaked	10g	20g	25g	30g	40g	45g	50g
Coconut grated	10g	25g	35g	40g	50g	60g	65g
Flour - all purpose (unsifted)	15g	30g	40g	45g	60g	70g	75g
Flour - cake	10g	20g	25g	30g	50g	60g	65g
Brown sugar	25g	50g	65g	75g	100g	125g	135g
Icing Sugar	15g	30g	40g	45g	60g	70g	75g
Sugar, granulated	30g	55g	75g	85g	115g	140g	150g

Volume Measurement (Fluids)

Milliliters	Tablespoons, Cups	Ounces
.5ml	a dash	
2.5ml	1/2 teaspoon	
5ml	1 teaspoon	
7.5ml	1 1/2 teaspoon or 1/2 tbsp	
10ml	2 teaspoons	
15ml	1 tablespoon	
30 ml	2 tablespoons	1 fluid ounce
60ml	4 tablespoons or 1/4 cup	2 fluid ounces
80ml	1/3 cup	
90ml	3/8 cup or 6 tablespoons	
125ml	1/2 cup or 8 tablespoons	4 fluid ounces
160ml	2/3 cup	
180ml	3/4 cup or 12 tablespoons	
240ml	1 cup or 16 tbsp or 1/2 pint	8 fluid ounces
375ml	1 1/2 cups	12 fluid ounces
480ml	2 cups or 1 pint	16 fluid ounces
960ml	1 quart or 2 pints	
1L (1000ml)	4 1/3 cups	
	.26 of a gallon	
	1 quart 2 ounces	
1.9 L	2 quarts or 1/2 gallon	
3.785L	4 quarts or 1 gallon	

Weight (Mass) Grams to Ounces

Grams	Ounces
15g	1/2 ounce
30g	1 ounce
85g	3 ounces
100g	3.75 ounces
115g	4 ounces
225g	8 ounces
340g	12 ounces
450g	16 ounces or 1 pound

Heat Conversion Table

°F = Degrees Fahrenheit   **°C = Degrees Celsius**

°F	°C		°F	°C		°F	°C
-40	-40		145	63		420	216
-30	-34		150	66		430	221
-20	-29		155	58		440	227
-10	-23		160	71		450	232
-5	-21		165	74		460	238
0	-18		170	77		470	243
5	-15		175	79		480	249
10	-12		180	82		490	254
15	-10		185	85		500	260
20	-6		190	88		510	266
25	-4		195	91		520	271
30	-1		200	93		530	277
32	0		205	96		540	282
35	2		210	99		550	288
40	4		212	100		560	293
45	7		220	104		570	299
50	10		230	110		580	304
55	13		240	116		590	310
60	16		250	121		600	316
65	18		260	127			
70	21		270	132			
75	24		280	137			
80	27		290	143			
85	29		300	149			
90	32		310	154			
95	35		320	160			
100	38		330	166			
105	41		340	171			
110	43		350	177			
115	46		360	182			
120	49		370	188			
125	52		380	193			
130	54		390	199			
135	57		400	204			
140	60		410	210			

Quick Equivalencies

Liquid

1ml	=	0.035 fluid ounces (fl oz)
30ml	=	1 fl oz
1US pint	=	16 fl oz
1UK pint	=	20 fl oz
500ml	=	16 fl oz = 2 cups
1 tsp	=	5ml
1 tbsp	=	15ml
1 liter	=	1 quart

Solid Weight

30g	=	1 oz
5 tbsp	=	1/3 cup

Glossary of Culinary Terms

A

À La, Au, Aux: French term meaning "served with" or "served in the manner."

À la bourguignonne: Refers to a dish or item prepared in Burgundy.

À la carte: Refers to a list of food items each priced separately.

À la crème: Served with cream or a cream-based sauce.

À la française: A term of reference, meaning "in the French style."

À la maison: Denotes a dish that is "home made," or a dish that is unique to the place of service.

À la mode: Served with or in the fashion of. Desserts served *à la mode* are served with ice cream; meats served *à la mode* are braised with vegetables and served with gravy.

Acidify: To add lemon juice, lime juice, or vinegar to a liquid.

Aging: Holding meats at a temperature of 34° to 36° Fahrenheit for a period of time to break down the tough connective tissues through the action of enzymes, thus increasing tenderness.

Al dente (al-den-tay): An Italian term, usually referring to pasta. It is used to describe the texture of slight resistance when bitten. In Italian it means "to the tooth." For the best flavor, cook pasta until it is firm and chewy.

Artichoke: The globe artichoke is the bud of a large plant in the thistle family with tough petal-shaped leaves. When properly cooked, break off the leaves one by one, dip in butter or sauce, and draw the base of the leaf through your teeth scraping off the pulp and discarding the rest of the leaf. At the center, scrape off the tiny leaves and fuzz and then continue to dip and eat the heart of the artichoke. The Jerusalem artichoke is not a true artichoke but a tuber resembling a ginger root. These may be used peeled or unpeeled, raw as an addition to salads, or steamed or boiled as a side dish.

Arugula: A bitter and aromatic salad green. Good source of iron and vitamins A and C.

Asparagus: A green, fern-like perennial plant and member of the lily family. The spears we eat are actually the shoots from an underground crown. Asparagus can be served hot or cold.

Au jus: Served in unthickened natural juices or natural meat drippings.

Au poivre: A classic sauce, finished with peppercorns, brandy and cream.

Au vin blanc: A dish cooked with, or containing, white wine.

B

Baguette: A long, narrow loaf of French bread, usually with a crispy brown crust and a soft, but chewy interior. Baguettes are noted for their very crispy crust and slightly buttery taste.

Bain-marie: A water bath, either hot or cold, used to help control the temperature of an item.

Bake: To cook in an enclosed oven.

Baking powder: A leavener containing baking soda, an acid (such as cream of tartar), and a moisture-absorber (such as cornstarch). Double-acting baking soda releases carbon dioxide gas when it becomes wet and again when exposed to oven heat. To test baking powder's effectiveness, mix 1 teaspoon baking powder with 1 cup hot water and the mixture should bubble immediately.

Balsamic vinegar: A fragrant vinegar made from the juice of Trebbiano grapes. The juice is heated and aged in wooden barrels, evaporating and concentrating in flavor. The resulting vinegar is deep rich brown with a sweet and sour flavor.

Basil: A member of the mint family with a pungent flavor. A popular herb in Mediterranean cooking and a primary ingredient in Italian pesto, used both fresh and dried.

Bass: A white sea fish of three varieties—silver, sea, and striped—sold as steaks and fillets. Can be barbecued, grilled, steamed, poached, or baked. Good with strong flavorings.

Baste: To moisten with the pan juices or other liquid during cooking. This aids in moisture retention. (Caution: Basting tools, such as brushes and bulb basters, could be sources of bacteria when uncooked or undercooked meat juices come in contact with them and they sit at room temperature, then are used again for basting.)

Batter: Wet, uncooked mixture that can be spooned or poured.

Bay leaf: An aromatic leaf that comes from bay laurel. Used whole, halved, or ground. It lends a slightly bitter, pungent seasoning to soups, stews, and stocks.

Beef fillet (filet mignon): This tender but expensive boneless cut of meat comes from the small end of the tenderloin. It should be cooked quickly by grilling or sautéing. Not an overly flavorful cut of meat.

Beef stock: Real beef stock is superior, but consommé or bouillon (mostly salt) may be substituted in a pinch.

Béarnaise: This is the most notable of all the hollandaise sauce variations. It is made with a wine and vinegar reduction flavored with tarragon.

Beat: To introduce air into a mixture using a utensil such as a wooden spoon, fork or whisk in order to achieve a lighter texture.

Bell peppers: Also known as sweet peppers. Bell peppers are "mature" when they turn bright green, but they are not yet ripe; their flavor is sharp, even acrid at this point. If picked after they have ripened to red, yellow, or orange their flavor will have mellowed considerably.

Beurre blanc: An emulsified sauce made of a wine or vinegar reduction blended with softened butter. It is flavored different ways for fish, vegetables, and poultry dishes.

Bisque: A rich shellfish soup made with the shells of an animal. The soup is enriched with cream and cognac and garnished with pieces of the shellfish meat. This name is also used to describe vegetable soups prepared in the same manner as shellfish bisques.

Blanch: To briefly plunge food into boiling water or hot fat.

Blend: To mix together ingredients, usually of different consistencies, to a smooth and even texture, utilizing a utensil such as a wooden spoon or blender.

Boeuf: The French term for beef.

Boil: To bring a liquid to boiling temperature and maintain it throughout the cooking time. The boiling point of water at sea level is 212°F and for every 500-foot increase in elevation, the boiling point drops one degree.

Bolognaise: A classic Italian meat sauce made from minced beef, onions, garlic, tomatoes, basil, oregano, and thyme.

Boning knife: A thin-bladed knife used for separating raw meat from the bone; its blade is usually about 6 inches long.

Boning: Preparation process that removes bones from meat, poultry, game, or fish.

Boston lettuce: This simple lettuce sports soft but fairly well-defined heads with lots of loose outer leaves. The bland tenderness mingles nicely with some bitter leaf lettuce and super-crisp romaine.

Bouquet garni: A sachet of herbs containing leeks, celery, parsley, thyme, black peppercorns, and bay leaf. Variations may include rosemary, marjoram, and fennel.

Braise: To bake or stew food slowly in a small amount of liquid, usually on a bed of vegetables in a covered pan or ovenproof dish.

Braising: A cooking method where food (usually meat) is first browned in oil, then cooked slowly in a liquid (wine, stock, or water).

Brioche: A very rich bread made with butter and eggs. Brioche is baked in many shapes, though the brioche en tête is best known. The dough can be flavored with nuts or candied fruit, as well as herbs and spices. It may also be used to wrap foods.

Broil: To cook at a measured distance below direct, dry heat.

Brown: To fry in very shallow fat over a high heat in order to color the food and seal in the juices. This is usually a very quick process, not more than a couple of minutes on each side.

Brulée: Finishing method applied to dishes such as cream custards finished with caramelized sugar glaze. Can be done with a torch or under the broiler.

Button mushroom: The standard, white, cultivated mushroom. Button mushrooms work well in concert with wild mushrooms, which are more intensely flavored, but also more expensive.

C

Cabbage: A vegetable that is a member of the Brassica vegetable group. Round in shape and heavy in weight, cabbages range from white in color to green to red and purple.

Caesar salad: This world famous salad combines crisp lettuce, crisp bacon pieces, croutons, and a white cream dressing made from Parmesan cheese, garlic, parboiled eggs, and anchovies.

Camembert cheese: A soft, fresh white rind cheese covered in white molded skin. Ripe camembert has a soft and "runny" texture when served at room temperature.

Candy thermometer: A kitchen gadget used to determine heat levels in the cooking of candy, jams, and preserves.

Cayenne pepper: A fiery hot ground spice derived from the flesh and seeds of chili pepper.

Celeriac: A tuberous root with brown gnarly skin, white fibrous flesh, and a mild celery flavor.

Celery: A shoot vegetable with long ribbed stems and green leaves. The leaves are often used in stocks and the most common varieties are Pascal and Golden celery.

Champagne: Sparkling wine, produced in France.

Chef, commis: The assistant chef to the chef de partie.

Chef, sous: The second chef, or second in command, to the head chef.

Chef boulangere: The chef responsible for the bakery section.

Chef chocolatier: The chef responsible for the section that handles the production of chocolate and confectionery items.

Chef de cuisine: Head chef, responsible for the overall operation of the kitchen.

Chef de partie: Chef responsible for the operation of a kitchen station.

Chef de rang: Chef de rang is the senior waiter who reports to the station head waiter within a restaurant.

Chef entremetier: The chef responsible for the production of vegetable dishes and vegetable accompaniments (side dishes).

Chef garde-manger: Chef responsible for the production of entrées and garnishes.

Chef pâtissier: Chef responsible for the section that prepares dessert items.

Chef poissonier: Chef responsible for the section that prepares fish dishes.

Chef potager: Chef responsible for the section that prepares soups.

Chef rôtisseur: Chef responsible for the section that roasts meats and prepares soups.

Chef saucier: Chef that produces the stocks and sauces to accompany each dish.

Chef tournant: Replacement or relief chef, who must replace anyone who is absent from the brigade. If no one is absent, the chef tournant may assist the kitchen brigade wherever they are required.

Chèvre: The French word for "goat" has come to refer to goat's cheese. Chèvres can vary in maturity (and strength of flavor) and range in texture from moist and creamy to dry and semi-firm. They come in a variety of shapes including cylinders, disks, cones, and pyramids and are often coated in edible ash or leaves, herbs, or pepper.

Chicken: One of the principal kinds of poultry; any of several varieties of common domestic fowl, used for food as well as egg production; has both light and dark meat and relatively little fat.

Chive: A member of the onion family, this fragrant herb has slender, vivid green, hollow stems. Chives have a mild onion flavor and are available fresh year-round. They are a good source of vitamin A and also contain a fair amount of potassium and calcium.

Cilantro: The North American term for coriander.

Coarsely chop: To cut food into small pieces, about 3/16 inches square.

Compote: A dish of fruits, stewed or baked, whole or in pieces, with sugar.

Concasser: To chop roughly.

Consommé: Clear broth that is made from meat.

Convection cooking: Convection ovens use a small fan in the rear of the oven to circulate air all around the food to cook it quickly and more evenly. Cooking times are generally reduced by 25%. Most manufacturers suggest that you reduce the cooking temperature given in the recipe by 25° and bake it for the time specified.

Convection oven: An electric oven in which heat is circulated rapidly around the cooking foods by means of a fan, resulting in fast crisping and browning.

Coriander: Coriander is the world's most commonly used herb. Both the fresh leaves and seeds are used. The herb has a fresh taste, similar to orange, and is an important ingredient in curry.

Cream: A component of milk with a milkfat content of at least 18%. It is more viscous and richer tasting than milk and can be whipped to a foam (whipped cream). It rises to the top of raw milk.

Crème fraîche: A naturally thickened fresh cream that has a sharp, tangy flavor and rich texture. This is an expensive item to buy, but a good substitute can be made by mixing heavy cream with uncultured buttermilk, and allowing to stand well covered in a tepid place until thickened.

D

Deep fryer: An appliance used for deep-frying food items in hot oil or fat.

Deep fry: To cook food by fully immersing it within hot oil or fat heated to 170°–180° C.

Deglaze: To use a liquid such as stock, water, or wine to dissolve food particles that are left in a pan after roasting or frying.

Demi-glace: Thick and intense meat flavored gel. Made by reducing stock to a syrupy liquid.

Descaling fish: Removing the scales from a fish, which is best done by first cutting off the fins and then, holding on to the tail, scraping away the scales in an upwards motion with the back of a knife, working towards the head, followed by rinsing.

Dijon: A French prepared mustard made in the Dijon region from black or brown mustard seeds, blended with salt, spices, and white wine or verjuice. Has a clean, sharp, medium-hot flavor; yellow-gray color; and creamy texture.

Dill: A member of the parsley family. The feathery leaves have a parsley-like flavor with overtones of anise and are used fresh or dried as an herb. The flat, oval, brown seeds have a slightly bitter caraway-like flavor, also with overtones of anise and are used as a spice.

Drippings: The fat, juices, and other residues separated from meat during cooking and left in the pan, or crusted onto the bottom of the pan.

Du jour: A French term meaning "of the day," a dish prepared especially for the day.

Duxelles: A thick pâté of chopped mushrooms cooked with onion, thyme, and white wine. Duxelles is used as a stuffing or garnish and in the preparation of various dishes called *à la duxelles*. Traditionally used in Beef Wellington.

E

Egg: The ovoid, hard-shelled reproductive body produced by a bird, consisting principally of a yolk and albumen. It is a good source of protein, iron, sulfur and vitamins A, B, D, and E, but also relatively high in cholesterol.

En papillote: A method of cooking in which food is wrapped, sealed, and cooked, usually in greaseproof paper or tin foil.

F

Fat: A substance generally comprising glycerol and fatty acids.

Fennel: Aromatic plant, both with pale green, celery-like stems and bright green, feathery foliage. Its greenish-brown seeds and leaves have a strong aniseed flavor that complements fish, especially oily varieties such as mackerel or herring.

Fillet: Meat or fish that has no bones.

Filet mignon: A small cut of beef taken from the end of the fillet, considered by many to be the most elegant steak of all. It is very tender and sweet, but lacks the flavor of a steak with bone in.

Filo pastry: Thin sheets of pastry commonly used in Greek, Eastern European, and Middle Eastern cuisines. As the sheets are very thin, working quickly to prevent drying out is essential, and fillings, sweet or savory, should be almost cooked before use as the pastry only requires a short cooking time.

Fines herbes: French for "fine herbs," usually a mixture of parsley, chives, tarragon, and chervil used to flavor omelets, casseroles, and soups.

Foie gras: The rich pâté made from the liver of ducks and geese that have been force-fed and fattened until their livers become enlarged. It is a great French delicacy and very expensive. After preparation, the livers are marinated in armagnac, port, or madeira, depending on the chef's recipe. They are then stuffed with black truffle, pressed into a terrine, sprinkled with salt and sealed.

Food processor: This kitchen appliance originated from France. It consists of a sturdy plastic work bowl that sits on a motorized drive shaft. The cover of the bowl has a feed tube through which foods can be added. The food processor can easily chop, dice, slice, shred, grind, and purée most food in an efficient and speedy manner.

Fry: To cook over brisk heat in oil or fat to obtain a good seal and color.

G

Garlic: Strong scented bulb of a plant related to the onion. A clove is a small segment.

Garnish: To decorate a finished dish with extra items such as parsley, lemon wedges, etc.

Gingerroot: Gingerroot is a gnarled, brown root. Side branches have a milder, tangy ginger flavor than the main root, which can have a hot "bite." Grate unpeeled gingerroot, or peel and chop or slice, to add flavor to foods such as stir-fries, sauces, and baked goods.

Gluten: Elastic protein present in flour, providing most of the structure of baked products.

Gratin: Any dish that is topped with cheese or breadcrumbs, mixed with bits of butter and then heated in the oven or under the broiler until brown and crispy.

Grill: To cook foods above a heat source such as gas or electricity.

H

Herbs: Leafy, aromatic parts of a plant, which are used for seasoning.

Hors d'oeuvres: French term for small portions of food served as appetizers

J

Julienne: Food that is cut into thin strips to a thickness of approximately 1/8 inch and a length ranging from 1 to 2 inches.

L

Lardon: A strip of bacon or pork used to lard meat.

Leek: A relative of onions and garlic. It has a mild onion flavor and is used as a vegetable or as seasoning for salads, soups, and other dishes.

Loose leaf lettuce: Loose leaf lettuce varieties include green leaf, oak leaf, and red leaf. These varieties of lettuce offer large loose heads of crisp, delicately flavored leaves. More perishable than iceberg or romaine.

M

Marinade: A mixture of wet and/or dry ingredients used to flavor or tenderize food prior to cooking.

O

Olive oil: A mono-unsaturated fat pressed from tree-ripened olives. Olive oils are graded according to their acidity. "Extra virgin" is about 1% acid and is considered the finest. The other grades are superfine, fine, and virgin.

Onion: This underground bulb is related to leeks, garlic, and chives and is prized for its distinct, pungent flavor and aroma. There are two types: green ("scallions") and dry onions. The white-skinned onion has the mildest flavor.

Oregano: A popular culinary herb of the mint family with a flavor similar to that of sweet marjoram or thyme. Also called "wild marjoram." Oregano is not quite as sweet and has a stronger flavor than marjoram.

Organic food: In common usage, *organic* refers to foods cultivated and processed without fertilizers, insecticides, artificial coloring, artificial flavorings, or additives.

Oyster: A bivalve mollusk with a rough gray shell. The flesh varies from creamy beige to pale gray, the flavor from salty to bland, and the texture from tender to firm. The Atlantic, or

Eastern, oysters are considered superior to Pacific varieties.

P

Parboil: To partially cook food by boiling, prior to another method of cooking.

Pare: To cut off the skin or outer covering of a fruit or vegetable with a small knife.

Parchment paper: A grease- and heat-resistant paper used to line baking pans.

Poach: To cook food in hot liquid over a gentle heat so the liquid is barely bubbling.

Purée: To process food by means of mashing, sieving, or processing in a food processor until very smooth.

Q

Quahaug: Atlantic Coast clam.

Quail: A game bird of the partridge family that resembles a small, plump chicken.

Quenelle: A poached dumpling (oval), usually made of veal or chicken.

Quiche: This dish originated in the Alsace-Lorraine region of France. It is a pastry shell filled with a savory custard of eggs, cream, onions, mushrooms, meats, shellfish, and seasonings. Quiche Lorraine includes crisp bacon.

Quince: The round pear-shaped fruit of the quince tree. The flesh tastes somewhat like a cross between an apple and a pear. Popular in jams, jellies, and preserves, this fruit is normally better when cooked.

R

Reconstitute: To bring a concentrated or condensed food to its original strength by adding a liquid.

Reduce: To boil a liquid rapidly in order to decrease its volume by evaporation and produce a concentrated flavor and thicker consistency.

Refresh: To plunge food into, or run under, cold water after blanching to prevent further cooking.

Rice vinegar: A mild-flavored vinegar made from fermented rice.

Roast: To cook food in an oven or on a spit over a fire.

Rind: The skin or outer coating.

Roux: An equal mixture of flour and fat, cooked from pale to a golden brown. Used for thickening in sauces, soups, or stews.

Rubbing in: The incorporation of fat into flour. Butter is softened and cubed then gently rubbed between the thumb and forefinger, lifting the mix at the same time, until the fat is fully incorporated and the mixture resembles fine breadcrumbs in appearance.

S

Salsa: Sauce made from chopped tomatoes, onions, chilies, and cilantro.

Sauté: The cooking of food in a small amount of fat, preferably in a single layer, until it browns and softens. Small items are cooked uncovered, but larger pieces may need covering after the initial browning to complete the cooking. The pan is shaken over high heat to move the food around and prevent sticking. It is important not to overfill the pan.

Scald: To heat a liquid, usually milk, until it is almost boiling at which point very small bubbles begin to form around the edge of the pan.

Score: To make shallow incisions with a small knife on the surface of foods, either with parallel lines or criss-cross patterns in order to improve its appearance or to absorb the flavors of bastes and marinades. Also aids in even cooking.

Sear: To brown the surface of food in fat over high heat before finishing cooking by another method. Adds flavor.

Sea salt: Salt derived from the evaporation of sea water.

Season:
1) To season a pan, rub the inside of a clean pan with a good layer of oil, bake in the oven at 300° for an hour. Wipe off the excess oil. Do this a few times to build up the layer. 2) To add flavorings, herbs, spices etc. to foods.

Season to taste: Usually refers to adding extra salt and pepper.

Shallow-fry: To cook in oil that is no more than 1.25cm (1/2 inch) deep.

Shred: To tear or cut food into thin strips.

Shrimp paste: A seasoning made from dried shrimp that has been pounded into a paste.

Shuck: Remove shells from seafood or husks from corn.

Sieve: To separate liquids from solids, usually using a sieve.

Sift: To pass a dry ingredient, such as flour, through a sieve to ensure it is lump free.

Simmer: To cook food at a temperature just below boiling.

Skewer: Long metal or wooden sticks that are inserted into meat or vegetables for grilling.

Skim: To remove impurities from the surface of a liquid, such as stock, during or after cooking.

Skin: The removal of skin from meat, fish, poultry, fruit, nuts, and vegetables.

Slice: To cut food, such as bread, meat, fish, or vegetables, into flat pieces of varying thickness.

Snip: To cut fresh herbs or dried fruit with shears into small uniform pieces using short, quick strokes.

Soba noodles: Made from wheat and buckwheat flour. Roughly as thick as spaghetti and prepared in various hot and cold dishes.

Soy milk: Liquid pressed from ground soybeans.

Spices: Seasonings for food.

Steam: The cooking of food, over rapidly boiling water or other liquid. The food is usually suspended above the liquid by means of a trivet or steaming basket, although in the case of puddings, the basin actually sits in the water.

Steep: To soak food in a liquid such as alcohol or syrup until saturated.

Stew: To cook food in liquid on a stove top.

Stir-fry: To fry small pieces of food quickly in a large frying pan or wok over a high heat using very little fat and constantly moving the food around the pan throughout cooking.

Strain: To separate liquids from solids by passing through a sieve, muslin, or similar item.

Stock: Strained liquid in which meat, poultry, or fish has been simmered.

Sugar: Sweetener made from sugar beets or sugar cane.

Sweat: To cook food in a covered pan in a small amount of fat so the natural juices run into the pan. Foods cooked in this way will soften but not brown.

T

Tahini: Flavoring made from ground sesame seed, used in Middle Eastern countries.

Tallow: The harder and less fusible fat in animals and vegetables.

Tamari: Sauce made from soybeans, a thicker mellower cousin of soy sauce.

Tamarind paste: Asian flavoring that comes from the fruit of the tamarind tree. Tamarind is used in a wide range of Thai recipes to add sour flavor.

Tangelo: A cross between a tangerine and the pomelo. This fruit contains only a few seeds and provides a juicy, sweetly tart, taste.

Tangerine: A thin-skinned citrus fruit descended from the mandarin orange. It has a delicate, somewhat spicy, tart taste. Named after the African city of Tangiers (even though they originated in China).

Tapioca: A starchy granular food prepared from cassava and used in puddings. The name comes from the Brazilian word *tipioca*, which translates as juice of cassava. The tapioca is obtained by pulping the root, washing it out, and collecting the starch, which is then dried on heated plates.

Tarpon: A large, powerful game fish from the warmer waters of the Atlantic Ocean.

Tarragon: A distinctive, aromatic perennial herb often called "French tarragon." Used in butter, chowders, juices, marmalades, fish, poultry,

meat, soups, vegetables, and sauces. A little of this spice goes a long way.

Tartar sauce: A creamy, white sauce composed of mayonnaise, minced capers, dill pickles, onions or shallots, olives, lemon juice or vinegar, and other seasonings. Tartar sauce is often served as an accompaniment to fried fish.

Tea: Dried tea leaves were used 4,000 years ago in China to flavor water that had been boiled (to make it safe). Americans invented tea bags and iced tea. All tea is derived from a single plant species. The climate, soil, and processing creates the individual characteristics.

Tempura: A Japanese specialty prepared by deep frying fish and vegetables that have been dipped in tempura batter. The cooked batter is light, thin, and crispy. Usually served with rice and soy sauce.

Tender greens: An herb of the mustard family whose leaves are cooked and eaten like spinach. Americans cultivate this plant for its leaves. Asians cultivate it for its thick, tuberous crown, which they pickle. Also called mustard greens.

Teriyaki sauce: A Japanese sauce made of soy sauce, sake or sherry, sugar, ginger, and seasonings. Used as a marinade for chicken and beef. The sugar often gives the sauce a slight glazed appearance.

Thickeners: Food substances to give thicker consistency to sauces, gravies, etc.

Thyme: Thyme is a member of the mint family of herbs. It is used frequently in bouquet garni and is a popular herb used for flavoring soups, sauces, meat, poultry, fish, vegetables, and pasta. Thyme has a strong pungent flavor and is best used with restraint. Thyme is said to aid in the digestion of fats, making it an excellent complement for meat dishes.

Tilefish: This low-fat Atlantic fish is delicately flavored and has a flesh that is firm yet tender. Available fresh and frozen in steaks and fillets. Suitable for just about any cooking method.

Tilsit cheese: A cheese that was accidentally created when Dutch immigrants were trying to make gouda. This mild cheese is made from pasteurized milk. A very strong type called Farmhouse Tilsit is made from raw milk and aged 5 months.

Timbale: A dish of minced meat or fish cooked in a drum-shaped mold of pastry.

Toffee: A sweet of sugar, butter, and flavorings boiled together and then allowed to cool and harden.

Tofu: Also known as soybean curd, is a soft, cheese-like food made by curdling fresh hot soy milk with a coagulant.

Tokay: A famous wine from Tokay, a town in Hungary. Louis XIV said Tokay was "the wine of kings and the king of wines." Twenty eight villages in Hungary have the right to call the wine they produce "Tokay."

Tomatillo: A small fruit, also called the "Mexican tomato," that is related to the tomato and the cape gooseberry. The flavor is a mixture of lemons, apples, and herbs. Used in guacamole and many sauces.

Tomato: A fruit from the nightshade family (like the potato and eggplant). The U.S. government classified it as a vegetable for trade purposes in 1893. Tomatoes should not be refrigerated—the cold adversely affects the flavor and the flesh.

Tomato paste: The paste that results from cooking tomatoes for several hours, then straining and reducing them to a thick red, richly flavored concentrate.

Tomato purée: Tomatoes that have been cooked briefly, then strained.

Tomato sauce: A slightly thinner tomato purée, often mixed with seasonings for use in other sauces and dishes.

Tonic: Carbonated water that is sometimes flavored with fruit extracts, sugar, and a small amount of quinine, a bitter alkaloid. Tonic water is popular as a mix for alcohol beverages. It is also called quinine water.

Torsk: A large, saltwater fish related to the cod. It has firm, lean flesh. Also called cusk.

Torte: A rich, multi-layered cake made with little or no flour, but with ground nuts, breadcrumbs, eggs, sugar, and flavorings. The word *torte* is also used to describe some tart-like preparations.

Tortilla: A Latin American, thin, flat cake made of maize flour and baked on a flat piece of stone or iron.

Toss: To mix with a rising and falling action.

Tostada shell: A flat, crisp-fried flour or corn tortilla shell. This serves as the base upon which tostadas are created by adding refried beans, shredded chicken or beef, lettuce, tomatoes, cheese, sour cream, guacamole, and other ingredients.

Tournedos: A small piece of fillet beef, grilled or sautéed.

Treacle: An uncrystallized syrup produced when sugar is refined.

Tree oyster mushroom: This fan-shaped mushroom often grows on rotting tree trunks. This fungus is fairly robust and slightly peppery when raw but becomes much milder when cooked. Also known as "oyster mushroom."

Trifle: A sweet dish of sponge-cake flavored with wine or jam and topped with custard and whipped cream.

Tripe: The stomach lining of beef, pork, or sheep. Beef tripe is the most commonly available. Tripe is tough and requires long cooking.

Trout: A delicately flavored fish that belongs to the same family as salmon and whitefish. Most are freshwater, but some are marine (sea trout). The very popular rainbow trout, from California, has been introduced to many different countries.

Truss: To tie up meat or poultry with string before cooking in order to make a more compact shape for even cooking or to produce an appetizing appearance.

Turmeric: A slightly bitter spice taken from the root of a plant in the ginger family. Usually available ground, this spice is used to flavor baked goods, curries, fish, poultry, gravies, salads, and dressings.

Tuna: A saltwater fish related to the mackerel. Probably the most popular fish used in canning today. Tuna has a distinctive rich-flavored flesh that is moderately high in fat and a firmly textured, flaky, tender flesh.

Tunka: The melon-like fruit of a tropical Asian vine belonging to the gourd family. Also called "white gourd."

Turbinado sugar: A raw sugar that has been steam-cleaned. The coarse crystals are blond in color and have a delicate molasses flavor.

Turkey: An American game bird from the pheasant family that has been domesticated. Self-basting turkeys have been injected with butter or vegetable oil. "Roaster-fryers" (6–8 lb. birds) are becoming more popular for everyday fare.

Turnip: A cool-weather, white-fleshed root vegetable that is easy to grow. The so-called "yellow turnip" is actually a rutabaga. Choose smaller turnips because young turnips have a delicate, somewhat sweet flavor that becomes stronger with age.

Turnip greens: The green tops of the turnip plant. These greens start out slightly sweet, but become stronger tasting and tougher with age. They may be served boiled, sautéed, steamed, or stir-fried.

Turnip-rooted parsley: A parsley subspecies grown for its beige carrot-like root, which tastes somewhat like a cross between a carrot and celery. Used in stews and soups or eaten as a vegetable. Also called "parsley root."

Turtle beans: Also known as "black beans" and "black turtle beans," these beans have black skin, cream-colored flesh, and a sweet flavor that forms the base for black bean soup.

Tybo cheese: A mild-flavored, Danish, cow's milk cheese. It features a cream-colored inside that is dotted with holes. This cheese goes well with sandwiches, salads, sauces, and many cooked dishes. Sometimes flavored with caraway seeds.

U

Udon: Japanese word for "noodle."

Unsaturated fat: A kind of fat that is in liquid form at room temperature.

V

Valiant: A golden, slightly fruity bitter with a bitter hops flavor, from the Bateman brewery in Lincolnshire.

Vanilla: There are over 20,000 types of orchid, but only one produces anything edible—the vanilla plant. "Vanilla extract" comes from macerating beans

into an alcohol/water solution. "Imitation vanilla" comes from treated wood-pulp byproducts.

Veal: Calves that are slaughtered from 1 to 3 months of age. "Milk-fed" veal is produced from unweaned calves. "Bob veal" is under a month old; "baby beef" is 6 to 12 months old. To keep their flesh from darkening, these animals are not fed grains or grasses.

Vegetable marrow: This edible squash-like gourd, also known as "marrow squash," is related to the zucchini. It has a bland flavor and is often stuffed with a meat filling.

Vegetable oil: Any of a wide variety of non-animal oils. Most vegetable oils, with the exception of coconut and palm oils, are lower in saturated fats than animal-derived oils.

Vegetable oyster plant: Also known as "salsify," this biennial herb is cultivated for its root, which is used as a vegetable. Its flavor hints of a delicately flavored oyster. Can be found in North America in Spanish, Italian, and Greek markets.

Velouté: A sauce made with stock and cream, and thickened with a white roux.

Venison: This term covers the meat from antelope, caribou, elk, deer, moose, and reindeer. Venison is probably the most popular large game meat eaten today.

Verjuice: The harsh juice of the unripe grapes used in wine making.

Vermicelli: Italian for "little worms." Vermicelli is a very thin spaghetti-shaped pasta.

Vermouth: A white wine that has been steeped with an infusion of herbs, plants, roots, leaves, peels, seed, and flowers.

Viande: Meat.

Vinaigrette: A basic oil and vinegar dressing that includes salt and pepper. More elaborate variations include herbs, shallots, onions, mustard, and spices.

Vine spinach: An edible leaf from a tropical plant that is cultivated in certain parts of France. Vine spinach may be prepared in any manner appropriate for spinach. Also called "basella."

Vinegar: A weak solution of acetic acid and water used in pickling, preserving, tenderizing, and to add a sour flavor to foods.

Vodka: A clear, colorless, almost odorless unaged liquor made from potatoes and sometimes from corn, rye, or wheat.

W

Waffle: Pancake batter cooked in a special hinged cooking utensil called a "waffle iron," which cooks both sides at once and gives waffles their honey-combed, syrup-catching surface. Belgian waffles are often heaped with fruits and whipped cream.

Wakami: A dried seaweed. Wakami is soaked in cold water before it is served, often with cucumbers, miso, and vinegar. Also used in soups. Popular in Japanese cooking.

Waldorf salad: A salad made with apples, celery, nuts, whipped cream, and mayonnaise on a bed of lettuce.

Walnut oil: This expensive oil is pressed from walnuts and has a distinctive nutty flavor and fragrance. Used in salad dressings, sauces, baked goods, and for sautéing.

Wasabi: A Japanese horseradish that is dried, powdered, and made into a pale green paste with a sharp, pungent, extremely potent flavor. Often mixed with soy sauce and served as a condiment to sushi, sashimi, and other Japanese specialties.

Water chestnut: The nut-like kernel of a water plant that grows in southeast Asia. The flesh is white, crisp, and juicy and has a bland, somewhat sweet nutty flavor. Their crunchy texture makes them popular in stir-fried dishes.

Watercress: A member of the mustard family that grows in running water. Watercress has small, crisp, green leaves and a pungent flavor with a slightly bitter, peppery flavor. Use in salads, cream soups, and to garnish vegetables.

Watermelon: Originally from Africa, this melon has a sweet, moist, red flesh. Asians roast the seeds, and pickled watermelon rind is popular in some parts of the world.

Wax bean: A pale yellow variety of the green bean that is eaten with its pod.

Wheat: There are over 30,000 varieties of this ubiquitous grain. Cultivated for over 6,000 years, wheat is second only to rice as a grain staple. Wheat contains more gluten than other grains, making it an excellent choice for bread making.

Wheat bran: The rough outer covering of the wheat kernel. Wheat bran is low in nutritional value but high in fiber. Wheat bran is sold separately and is used to add flavor and fiber to baked goods.

Wheat cake: A pancake made of wheat flour.

Wheat flour: A flour produced by milling the endosperm portion of the wheat kernel. Whole wheat flour, which is more nutritious, is made by milling the entire kernel, including the outer covering, or bran.

Wheat germ: The tiny nucleus of the endosperm (the inner part of the wheat kernel without the outer bran). Wheat germ has a nutty flavor and is a concentrated source of oil, vitamins, minerals, and protein. Used to add nutrients to various foods.

Wheat gluten: The protein remaining after wheat flour has been washed to remove starch. Gluten helps hold in the gas bubbles produced by leavening agents. This is why bread flours contain high levels of gluten and cake flours contain low levels.

Wheat pilaf: A pilaf made from either the wheat berries (whole unprocessed kernels) or cracked wheat (the whole berries broken into coarse, medium, and fine parts).

Wheat, parboiled: A nutritious staple in the Middle East, made of wheat kernels that have been steamed, dried, and crushed. It has a tender, chewy texture and can be made into a pilaf. Also called "bulgur."

Whey: The liquid part of milk that remains after the curd is removed. Most whey is further separated, with the fattier parts used in making butter. Some whey is used to make "whey cheese" or "Ricotta cheese."

Whip: To beat an item, such as cream or egg whites, in order to incorporate air and thicken.

Whisk: To beat air into a mixture until soft and fluffy.

Whiskey: A liquor produced from the fermented mash of grains such as barley, corn, and rye. Popular varieties of whiskey include bourbon, Canadian whisky, Irish whiskey, rye, and scotch.

White bean: A generic term that refers to any of several dried beans, including marrow beans, great northern beans, navy beans, and "pea beans."

White chocolate: Not a true chocolate at all. It is a blend of sugar, cocoa butter, milk solids, lecithin, and vanilla. If a product does not contain cocoa butter, it isn't white chocolate.

White pepper: White peppercorn is somewhat less pungent than the black variety. After ripening, the skin is removed and the berry is dried. White pepper is used in light-colored sauces and dishes where black speckles could be unaesthetic.

White rice: Rice that has had the husk, bran, and germ removed. White rice is sometimes called "polished rice."

White sauce: A term for light, white, or blond sauces. In its simplest form, white sauce is cream or milk mixed into a white roux (a combination of butter and flour that isn't browned). This basic French sauce is called a béchamel sauce.

Whitefish: A high-fat, mild-flavored member of the salmon family with a firm, white flesh. The whitefish can be poached, baked, broiled, grilled, pan fried, or stuffed. Its roe (eggs) can be cooked or made into caviar by adding salt.

Whiting: A small gray and white saltwater fish sometimes called the silver hake. This low-fat fish, which is related to both the cod and the hake, has a tender, white, fine-textured flesh and a flaky, delicate flavor.

Wild rice: A plant from the same family as rice, but with a gray and brown grain that is about twice the length of ordinary rice grains. Wild rice has a unique, almost nutty flavor. Used to stuff game or poultry and served as a side dish.

Wine: An alcoholic beverage produced through the fermentation of grape juice. Other fruit and vegetable juices, such as dandelion and elderberry are also occasionally used in wine making, an art that goes back at least 12,000 years. Wine is the fermented juice of fruits, vegetables, or flowers. The more important wines are fermented from grapes. Can be white, red, or pink in color.

Winged bean: A fast-growing, high-protein legume. Also called the "goa bean." This bean is entirely edible, including the shoots, flower, roots, leaves, pods, and seeds. Tastes somewhat like a cross between the cranberry bean and the green bean.

Winter radish: A large plant thought to be of Oriental origin. These plants are grown chiefly for their pungent peppery root, which can grow to 2 pounds or more. This radish is popular in Germany and in the East. Also called "black radish."

Witloof chickory: The largest and most popular variety of chicory, a vegetable with long silvery-white leaves. Used in salads and as a seasoning.

Wolf fish: A firm, white-fleshed saltwater fish with a large head, strong jaws, and sharp canine teeth and molars that can grind clams, whelks, and other mollusks. Sometimes sold in North America under the confusing name of "ocean catfish."

Wonton skin: Paper-thin, round or square sheets of dough made from flour, eggs, and salt. Used as wrappers to make wontons and egg rolls. Wontons are small dumplings of thin dough around a minced mixture of meat, seafood, and/or vegetables.

Worcestershire sauce: This thin, dark sauce is made from garlic, soy sauce, tamarind, onion, molasses, lime, anchovies, vinegar, and seasonings. Used to season meats, gravies, soups, and vegetables. It was originally bottled in Worcester, England.

Y

Yam: There are over 150 varieties of yams grown throughout the world. Most "yams" sold in the U.S. are actually sweet potatoes. Yams are higher in sugar than sweet potatoes. Used in soups and stews, mashed, and fried.

Yam bean tuber: Large, bulbous, root vegetable with a thin, brown skin and a white, crunchy flesh with a texture similar to water chestnut. It has a sweet, nutty flavor and can be eaten raw or cooked. Also called "jicama."

Yardlong bean: A pencil-thin legume from the black-eye pea family that looks like a very long green bean. These beans can grow a yard long, but are usually picked at 18 inches or less. They are slightly less sweet and crispy than the green bean.

Yeast: A single-celled organism that breaks food down into alcohol and carbon dioxide in a process known as fermentation. Carbon dioxide gives beer and champagne effervescence and causes bread to rise.

Yellow fin tuna: These tuna reach about 300 pounds in weight. They feature a pale pink flesh that is relatively mild. Also called "ahi."

Yellowtail: A large game fish (up to 100 pounds) from the jack family with a flavor and texture resembling tuna. May be prepared in any manner suitable for tuna.

Yogurt: A curdled milk product made using acid and thickened by adding bacterial cultures. Fruit-flavored yogurts account for the biggest share of the yogurt market. Originated accidentally by nomadic Balkan tribes, then intentionally to preserve milk.

Yorkshire pudding: A batter made with flour, eggs, salt, and milk that is baked with standing rib roast (prime rib).

Youngberry: A hybrid variety of blackberry with a dark red color and a sweet, juicy flesh.

Yucca: A root with a crisp white flesh. There are two main categories of yucca: sweet and bitter. Bitter yuccas are toxic until cooked. Yucca is used to make cassreep and tapioca. Also called cassava.

Z

Zabaglione: An ethereal dessert made by whisking egg yolks, Marsala wine, and sugar over simmering water to convert the eggs into a foamy custard. Called sabayon in France.

Zester: A hand-held tool with small, sharp-edged holes at the end of it that cuts orange, lemon, or grapefruit peel into fine shreds.

Zinfandel: A dry, red wine with a fruity flavor that some compare to the flavor of raspberries.

Ziti: Macaroni that has been shaped into long, thin tubes.

Zucchini: Green Italian squash. A popular summer squash with an off-white flesh and a light, somewhat bland flavor. Zucchini can be steamed, grilled, sautéed, deep-fried, or baked.

Zwieback: "Zwieback" is the German word for "twice baked." Refers to bread that has been baked, then sliced and returned to the oven and cooked until very crisp and dry. Zwieback is popular for its easy digestibility.

Chapter Questions- Answer Key

Chapter 1
1. b
2. answers are: politics, social, climate, religion, technology, and availability of food.
3. France
4. c
5. d
6. Auguste Escoffier

Chapter 2
1. False- a kitchen team is called a "brigade"
2. d
3. Station Chef
4. Sous Chef
5. d- all are false statements regarding cooks.
6. answers are: Garde Manger / Pantry Chef Rotisseur / Roasting, Entremetier / Vegetable Chef, Grillardin / Grill, Chef Saucier / Sauce Chef, Poissonier / Fish Chef, Patissier / Pastry / Dessert Chef, Tournant / Replacement Chef

Chapter 3
1. b and c
2. True
3. False
4. get rested, get clean, good grooming
5. 52, the number of ways you can cook an egg

Chapter 4
1. a, c, d
2. b, c
3. know fire procedures / keep equipment clean / do not smoke / turn off all equipment when alarm sounds / keep exits clear / never leave cooking unattended
4. knees bent when lifting / use legs to lift, not back / stretch before and during shifts / avoid repetitive motions
5. d

Chapter 5
1. f- all of the above
2. to prevent sickness and ill health
3. wash hair, clean uniforms, wash hands
4. wash their hands
5. 30 seconds or longer
6. 41°-140°F, or 5°-60°C
7. hire a professional

Chapter 6
1. knives, pots, pans
2. delicate or detailed work
3. a convection oven has a fan that circulates air through the oven
4. measuring spoons, measuring cups, ladles, scales
5. False - a chef's most important tools are his hands

Chapter 7
1. dry heat, moist heat
2. a, c, d
3. a, b, d
4. False
5. 212° F or 100° C
6. The oil is absorbed into the food and renders it soggy and oily.
7. False- only stewed meats are always submerged. Braised meats are partially submerged.

Chapter 8
1. True
2. a, c, e
3. clean and sanitize the vegetable sink
4. e- all of the above
5. to soften meat fibers, to flavor meat
6. False- you always start with the flour
7. as a batter for fish in Fish & Chips

Chapter 9
1. True
2. d- all of the above
3. bad idea
4. 30 minutes before the end of the cooking process
5. basil, bay leaves, chives, coriander leaf, dill, marjoram, oregano, mint, parsley, rosemary, sage, tarragon
6. it is hand picked, and needs 75,000 crocus for 1lb.
7. Sea salt, Table salt
8. Anisette, pernod, ouzo, sambuca
9. Cherry

Chapter 10
1. False
2. e- all of the above
3. print error, misread instructions, unclear instructions, variable ingredients, etc.
4. False
5. weight, volume
6. True

Chapter 11
1. False
2. chicken, vegetable, brown, white, or fish
3. f- all of the above
4. to tie it to the pot handle so you can drop it in stocks and be able to remove it easily when you are finished using it
5. a and b
6. Glace de Viande (brown stock), Glace de Volaille (chicken stock), Glace de Poisson (fish stock)

Chapter 12
1. taste: lightness, richness; visual: texture, color
2. a, c, d
3. equal parts butter to flour
4. mornay, cream, mustard, soubise
5. a, b, c
6. b
7. c
8. garlic, hotel, herb, anchovy, curry, mustard, escargot, shrimp

Chapter 13
1. False
2. False
3. d
4. c
5. Avoid boiling the soup after the cream has been added
6. A chowder contains hearty pieces of meat, seafood, or vegetables, whereas a cream soup is generally smooth.

Recipe Index

Soups   139

Stocks   107

Various